Learn French for Travel

A complete guide for beginners to be fast in learning language with easy phrases and a simple vocabulary.

Paul Irving Educational

© Copyright 2019 by Paul Irving Educational - All rights reserved.

The content contained within this book may not be reproduced, duplicated or transmitted without direct written permission from the author or the publisher.

Under no circumstances will any blame or legal responsibility be held against the publisher, or author, for any damages, reparation, or monetary loss due to the information contained within this book. Either directly or indirectly.

Legal Notice:

This book is copyright protected. This book is only for personal use. You cannot amend, distribute, sell, use, quote or paraphrase any part, or the content within this book, without the consent of the author or publisher.

Disclaimer Notice:

Please note the information contained within this document is for educational and entertainment purposes only. All effort has been executed to present accurate, up to date, and reliable, complete information. No warranties of any kind are declared or implied. Readers acknowledge that the author is not engaging in the rendering of legal, financial, medical or professional advice. The content within this book has been derived from various sources. Please consult a licensed professional before attempting any techniques outlined in this book.

By reading this document, the reader agrees that under no circumstances is the author responsible for any losses, direct or indirect, which are incurred as a result of the use of information contained within this document, including, but not limited to, — errors, omissions, or inaccuracies.

Credits:

Image by **Freepik** - Freepik.com

Table of Contents

Table of Contents 4
Introduction 8
Chapter 1: Presentations and Greetings 15
   Vocabulary List for Chapter 1 21
Chapter 2: Knowing People/Nationality/Job 24
   Knowing People 24
   Nationalities 28
   Occupations 31
   Vocabulary List for Chapter 2 32
Chapter 3: Family 37
   Vocabulary List for Chapter 3 41
Chapter 4: Time/Days/Months/Seasons 45
   Time 45
   Days of the Week 51
   Months of the Year 53
   Years 54
   Dates 58
   Seasons 59
   Putting It All Together: Sentence Examples 59
   Vocabulary List for Chapter 4 61
Chapter 5: Weather 71
   Vocabulary List for Chapter 5 76
Chapter 6: Food 82

Groceries, *Épicerie* 83
    Staples, Agrafes.. 83
    Vegetables and Fruits 84
    Meat 85
Others/Dishes, *Autres/plats*... 87
Fast-Food 87
Putting It All Together: Sentence Examples........................ 89
Vocabulary List for Chapter 6 90

Chapter 7: Home.. 98
The Kitchen 99
The Bedroom 100
The Bathroom.. 101
The Living Room 101
Vocabulary List for Chapter 7 103

Chapter 8: Animals..108
House Animals/Pets...108
Farm Animals 109
Zoo Animals..109
Other Animals 111
More Sentence Examples.. 112
Vocabulary List for Chapter 8 113

Chapter 9: How to Ask for Information and Help With the Language 119
Vocabulary List for Chapter 9 125

Chapter 10: To Go Shopping 127
Vocabulary List for Chapter 10 132

Chapter 11: Restaurant/Coffee **136**
   Coffee Shop 143
   Vocabulary List for Chapter 11 145
   Answers to Chapter 11 Quiz 148

Chapter 12: Finding the Way/Directions **150**
   Addresses 150
      Streets.. *150*
      Numbers... *151*
   Address Examples.. 152
   À Washington vs. Au Washington............................. 153
   Asking for Directions 154
   Vocabulary List for Chapter 12 156

Chapter 13: Modes of Transportation **158**
   Example Sentences 160
   Vocabulary List for Chapter 13 161

Chapter 14: Travel, Transportation, and How to Book/Buy a Ticket **164**
   Buying a Ticket 164
   Checking In 166
   More Travel Words and Phrases 167
   Vocabulary List for Chapter 14 168

Chapter 15: Hotels and Accomodations **171**
   More Useful Hotel Terms 173
   Vocabulary List for Chapter 15 175

Chapter 16: At the Museum **177**
   Positive Descriptors... 178

Negative Descriptors 179
Phrases 179
Vocabulary List for Chapter 16 181

Chapter 17: Parts of the Body and Medical Emergency 185

Parts of the Body 185
Verbs Involving the Body 187
Visiting the Doctor 188
Words and Phrases for a Medical Emergency 189
Vocabulary List for Chapter 17 191

Chapter 18: Hobbies, Games, and Sports 196

Hobbies 196
Games 197
Sports 198

Vocabulary List for Chapter 18 200

Chapter 19: Conversations About the Future 204

Future Verbs 204
Future Sentences 205
Vocabulary List for Chapter 19 207

Conclusion 209

Introduction

Welcome to *Learn French for Travel*. This book is designed to help you begin your studies of conversational French and allow you to embark on travels to French-speaking countries with confidence.

This book is divided into different chapters based on the subject that it concerns. There are various topics covered, and each of them has different phrases for you to learn, including expressions on how to buy a ticket and order food in a restaurant.

Before we begin, I will give you a guide on how to use this book so that you get the best possible results. Each chapter contains a vocabulary list at the end, which you can easily go back to again and again on your travels if you forget a word or a phrase. As you know, the pronunciation of the words is important, so this vocabulary list will contain not only the keywords from the chapter but also the pronunciation of each. If you are reading a chapter and you get stumped with regards to how to pronounce a word, just flip to the list of vocabulary words at the end of the chapter and practice saying it aloud a few times to get the pronunciation right before continuing with your reading.

As you read through this book, including the phrases and the vocabulary list, read them aloud for the best results. Reading a new language or a language that you are practicing aloud will help you teach your brain and your mouth and tongue how to say the words correctly. Since you will use most of these phrases in a conversational setting, knowing how to say them aloud is the purpose, so why not practice speaking them while you read through the book?

Furthermore, repeating everything you read a few times over will allow it to sink into your brain and really help you to understand exactly what you are reading. Read each phrase aloud to yourself a few times over, and this will help you memorize the phrase and the order of the words, as well as your pronunciation and your understanding of the French language in general.

When it comes to learning a new language or learning anything new for that matter, repetition is key to success. The more you repeat these phrases, the more you will learn them. Then, when you are in France, and you need to buy a ticket for the train, the phrase will come back to you easily because of how many times you practiced saying it. This book is not one that you will read once and then never again; this book is meant to be read over and over again or flipped back to when you are looking for something specific. There is no number of times that would count as too much when reading this book, so keep practicing until you have memorized it all, and then read it again!

The method for reading this book is to under the rules and concepts when forming phrases in French, and then by repeating them over and over, you will eventually be equipped to create your own phrases or rearrange them to suit your needs. For example, if you learn how to ask someone for a ticket, then you will eventually be able to tell someone to get a ticket by combining your knowledge of the words "ticket" and "buy," as well as directional cues that you will also learn in this book. Through the basic rules and concepts in this book, you can then extrapolate them to become a conversational French language speaker!

One thing that French and English have in common is that they use the same alphabet. This makes it easier for English speakers to learn French as they already know the alphabet and just need to learn the differences in pronunciation between the languages. At the end of this chapter, we will look at the pronunciation of the French alphabet.

There are some notable differences between the French and English languages. The first and most noticeable difference is that instead of referring to *the* or *a*, like we do in English, in French, there are different forms of these two words so you can say *la, le, les, des, de la,* and so on. You will see more examples of this throughout the book, but knowing which to use is very important when it comes to speaking French so that the people you are talking to will know exactly what you are referring to.

The reason for all these different forms in French is that everything in the French language has an assigned gender. Now, this may sound odd, but it is true. Everything, from a chair to a kettle and in between, has an assigned gender, which informs the learner what forms of "*the*" or "*a*" you will use when speaking about them. In this book, you will be taught to say all of the words in the language of French, at the same time, as you learn their gender, so fear not; this will become easy for you eventually as you get used to the common words that you will be exposed to.

The other thing to note is that in French, there are changes that you need to make to a sentence if you are speaking to someone whom you want to show respect to or someone you are close to, like friends and family members. In English, we do not talk to a person differently if we want to show them respect; at most, we will address them with a more formal tone of voice. You will see examples of this in our first chapter.

Another notable difference between French and English is that, in English, we emphasize specific parts of words or sentences in order to convey the meaning of our sentence. By changing the word or the place in the sentence on which we place emphasis, we can change the meaning of our sentence. For example, the sentence below can have five different and subtle meaning changes based on which of the five words we emphasize when we are speaking.

You went home last night.

You went home **last** night.

You went **home** last night.

You **went** home last night.

You went home last **night**.

When it comes to speaking French, however, there is no emphasis placed on certain words to change the meaning. Instead, we change the order of our words to convey meaning. The reason for this is to have no chance of misunderstanding when speaking, as the order of the words will convey the message we are trying to get across. In French, we want the language to flow out of our mouths in a romantic and smooth-sounding way, and having emphasis will get in the way of this. It is important to ensure your words are in the proper order when you are speaking French so that you are conveying the message you want to convey and not accidentally meaning something different because of the order in which you said the words. You will see more examples of this in the chapters that follow, and by the end of the book, you should be quite comfortable with this concept.

Before we begin our first chapter, we are going to look at some simple pronunciations to get you started. Below are the letters of the alphabet and their pronunciations. There are some letters that have the same pronunciation in both French and English.

Those letters are as follows: F, L, M, N, O, and S. All of the other letters, however, have new and different pronunciations. Study them and learn their new pronunciations before moving on to the next chapter. Begin by reading these letters aloud with their appropriate names a few times over so that you can get used to these new ways of naming them.

The pronunciation of each letter is as follows:

A (ah), B (bay), C (say), D (day), E (euh), F (ef), G (jh-ay), H (ash), I (ee), J (jh-ee), K

(kah), L (el), M (em), N (en), O (oh), P (pay), Q (koo), R (err (roll the r)), S (ess), T (tay),

U (ooh), V (vay), W (doo-bl-uh-vey), X (ee-ks), Y (ee-greck (roll the r)), Z (zed).

As you know from speaking English, the pronunciation of letters can change when they are placed together with other letters. Their pronunciation can change depending on which letters come before and after them. Thus, we will look at the most common letter combinations in the French language and the sounds they produce. One thing to note is that some letter combinations will produce the same sounds. The reason for this is that they will be found in different words, so just keep this in mind as you read through the rest of this book. Practice the pronunciations of the common letter pairings and the sounds they form below.

Ai [eh]

Au [oh]

Eau [oh]

Eu [uh]

Ei [eh]

In [eh]

Ien [yeh]

O [oh]

Ou [oo]

On [aw]

Om [aw]

Oi [wah]

Un [eh]

Now that you are familiar with both the letter names and the common letter pairings, as well as their pronunciations, we will move on to the first chapter of this book. If you need a refresher as to how to say a certain letter pairing, flip the page back here at any time.

Chapter 1: Presentations and Greetings

Présentations et salutations

We are going to begin our first chapter by looking at common greetings that you will use in French when you first meet someone or when you encounter someone and begin a conversation. This will help you to know how to get a conversation started. All of the words italicized within the text here can be found in a vocabulary list at the end of the chapter. If you want to practice pronunciations of any phrase before you continue, flip to the end of the chapter before coming back to continue reading.

The first words we will begin with are *hello* and *hi*. You will use these quite often, so spend some time practicing this word and its pronunciation. In French, "hello" is *Bonjour* [bon-j-oor].

Another one that is similar to hello that you may use often is *Bonsoir* [b-ohn-s-wah], which means "good evening." This one can be used both formally and informally, depending on the circumstances.

There are a few other ways to say hello; some are less formal and more of a casual way to greet someone that is usually reserved only for your friends or family members. They are as follows:

- *Salut* [sah-loo], which can mean either hello or goodbye and is quite informal, like saying "hey" and "see ya," but with a single word that can be used anytime.
- *Coucou* [k-oo-k-oo] this one is a silly greeting that means "hey!" for close friends and people like your siblings.
- *Allô* [ah-loh], which is usually used when you pick up a phone call or when you call someone. This is primarily used in Canadian French; it is a sort of combination of both English and French in one.

If you are meeting someone for the first time, you would say, *Je m'appelle* [j-uh][m-ah-p-el]. This directly translates to "I am called." You would say *Je m'appelle* _____ (insert your name).

To introduce someone else, like if you bring a friend to a party or something of the sort, you would say, *Je te présente* _____ (insert their name) [j-uh][tuh][pr-eh-s-on-tuh]. If you want to say this more formally like if you are introducing someone in a work-related meeting, you would say *Je vous présente* _____ (insert their name) [j-uh][v-oo][pr-eh-s-on-tuh].

If you want to inquire about someone's name, you would say one of two things. Remember how, in the introduction to this book, I introduced the concept of addressing someone? You use different words depending on their relationship with you: if they are your friend or if they are an acquaintance to whom you want to show respect. This is where that concept is applicable, and I will show you the different options and examples of this.

Firstly, if you are speaking to a friend or someone who is deemed an equal of yours, you would say *Comment t'appelles-tu?* [k-ohm-on][t-app-el][too]. *Tu* is a less formal and more casual way of addressing a person. If, however, you want to show them respect or if they are an elderly or something like this, you would say, *Comment vous appelez-vous?* [k-ohm-on][v-oo-z][app-el-ay][v-oo]. In English, we would ask, "What is your name?" or "...and you are?" or something along those lines, regardless of who we are asking, but in French, this distinction is important.

After you have introduced yourself to someone and you have exchanged names, either you or the other person will say, *enchanté* [on-sh-on-tay], which is how we say, "Nice to meet you." It directly translates to mean, "Enchanted to meet you."

There are also a couple of other options that are more similar to what we would say in English, such as *C'est un plaisir de faire votre connaissance*, which uses the word "pleasure," meaning there is pleasure in meeting the person. Another way to say this is *C'est un plaisir de vous connaître*.

Whether you have just met someone or you meet up with someone whom you already know, you can ask them how they are by saying, *Comment allez-vous?* [coh-mon][ah-lay][v-oo-z], which means "how are you doing." This is a nice way of asking someone how they are doing. This would be used as a nicer and slightly more formal way of saying this, and if you want to ask your friend how they are, you can say something like "Hey, how are ya?" or "what's up?," and in French, you say, *Ca va?* [sah][vah]. This is used very commonly in French between friends as a replacement for "hi" and "how are you" at the same time, similar to what we would say in English.

If you want to ask someone specifically "What's new?" or "What's up?, you can ask this by saying *Quoi de neuf?* [k-wah][duh][n-uff], which directly translates to mean "What is new?" As a response to any of these, you can say the following:

Bien, et toi? Good, you? (less formal)

Bien, et vous? Good, you? (more formal)

Mal, et toi? Bad, you? (less formal)

Mal, et vous? Bad, you? (more formal)

Rien, toi? Nothing, you? (less formal)

Rien, vous? Nothing, you? (more formal)

As you begin the conversation with the person you have just met, you can say

Je suis [j-uh][s-wee], which means "I am." This would come in handy when you are getting to know someone, and you want to tell them more about yourself. This can be followed by just about anything that you want to say, for example, a feeling or an adjective, or it can simply begin a sentence. An example is below.

Je suis heureux [j-uh][s-wee][euh-r-uh], which means "I am happy"

You can also begin a sentence by saying what you do for work or by asking the person what they do. *Je travaille comme dentiste* means "I work as a dentiste" or *je suis dentiste* ("I am a dentist"). You can ask them by saying, *quoi est-ce que vous faites comme travail?*, which uses the formal tone since it uses *vous*. To say this casually, you can use the question: *qu'est ce que tu fais comme travail?* You will see more about occupations in another chapter in this book.

You will likely also need to know how to say yes or no since, in a conversation, the other person will probably ask you at least a couple of yes-or-no questions.

Oui [wee], yes

Non [noh], no

If you are initiating a conversation with someone to whom you have not been introduced, you can get their attention by saying, *excusez-moi* [ex-k-you-z-ay][m-wah], which translates to "excuse me."

This is a polite or cautious way of attracting someone's courtesy, and it can also be used to ask someone to move aside politely if you need to pass through or if they are in your way. From this, a conversation may ensue, which is when you would introduce yourself and ask them how they are doing, as you have learned above.

Like most languages, there are at least two ways of saying things: formal and informal. In the case of "please" in French, the formal and informal ways depend on the pronoun, e.g., "you." As you learned previously, there are two ways to say *you*. The word *vous* means "you" and is used in a much more formal way than *tu*. *Vous* can also be used in a plural sense to talk about people in terms of "you as a pair" or "you as a group" of people. If you have just met someone or if they are someone whom you want to show respect and be more formal with, then you will use the first example below. If you are friends with them and you want to say *please* in a more casual and less formal way, then you can use the second one.

S'il vous plaît [seel][v-oo][play], please

S'il te plaît [seel][t-uh][play], please

For example, you can put this together with the previous phrase to say, "excuse me, please" by saying *excusez-moi s'il vous plaît*.

Vocabulary List for Chapter 1

In this vocabulary list, you will find the most important words from the chapter laid out for you, along with their pronunciations. This list will be an easy way for you to look up certain phrases when you need them and to practice the pronunciation of words that you have trouble with. All of the words in this list can be found italicized within the chapter.

Présentations et salutations

Bonjour [bon-j-oor], hello

Bonsoir [b-ohn-s-wah]. Good evening.

Salut [sah-loo], hey or bye

Coucou [k-oo-k-oo], heyyo

Allô [ah-loh], hi (on the phone)

Je m'appelle... [j-uh][m-ah-p-el]. My name is...

Je te présente [j-uh][tuh][pr-eh-s-on-tuh]. This is (so and so)

Je vous présente [j-uh][v-oo][pr-eh-s-on-tuh]. This is (so and so)

Comment t'appelles-tu? [k-ohm-on][t-app-el][too]. What is your name?

Comment vous appelez-vous? [k-ohm-on][v-oo-z][app-el-ay][v-oo]. What is your name?

All three phrases/sentences translate to *"Pleasure to meet you."*

- *Enchanté [on-sh-on-tay]*
- *C'est un plaisir de faire votre connaissance [say][uhn][pl-eh-zee-r][duh][fair][v-oh-t-ruh][k-on-ay-s-oh-n-s]*
- *C'est un plaisir de vous connaître [say][uhn][pl-eh-zee-r][duh][voo][k-on-eh-t-ruh]*

Comment allez-vous? [coh-mon][ah-lay][v-oo-z]. How are you?

Ça va? [sah][vah]. How are ya doing?

Quoi de neuf? [k-wah][duh][n-uff]. What's new?

Bien, et toi? [bee-yeh][eh][t-wah]. Good, and you?

Bien, et vous? [bee-yeh][eh][v-oo]. Good, and you?

Mal, et toi? [mah-l][eh][t-wah]. Bad, and you?

Mal, et vous? [mah-l][eh][v-oo]. Bad and you?

Rien, toi? [r-ee-yeh](rolled r)[t-wah]. Nothing, you?

Rien, vous? [r-ee-yeh](rolled r)[v-oo]. Nothing, you?

Je travaille comme dentiste [j-uh][t-rah-v-eye][k-oh-m][d-on-tee-s-t]. I work as a dentist.

What is your work/livelihood?

- *Quoi est-ce que vous faites comme travail? [k-ess][suh][k-uh][v-oo][f-eh-tuh][k-uhm][t-rah-v-eye]*
- *Quoi est-ce que tu fais comme travail? [k-ess][suh][k-uh][t-oo][f-ay]][k-uhm][t-rah-v-eye]*

Je suis dentiste [j-uh][s-wee][d-on-tee-s-t]. I am a dentist.

Oui [wee], yes

Non [noh], no

Excusez-moi [ex-k-you-z-ay][m-wah]. Excuse me.

S'il vous plaît [seel][v-oo][play], please

S'il te plaît [seel][t-uh][play], please

Excusez-moi s'il vous plaît [ex-k-you-z-ay][m-wah][seel][v-oo][play]. Excuse me, please.

Chapter 2: Knowing People/Nationality/Job

Connaître les gens, la nationalité et l'emploi

The focus of this chapter will be on people and the titles we can use to describe them. Remember, I outlined the fact that everything in French has an assigned gender in the introduction of this book? This will be evident in this chapter as the words will be preceded by an article, such as *le, la, des,* and *de la,* which are different ways of saying *the* or *a* but which have associated genders. Along with this will be either an (e) or an (s), which means that if it is someone female you are talking about, you will add the *e*, and if it is plural, like a group of people, you will add the *s*.

Knowing People

This section will focus on people you know in your life and what you would call them in French. We are going to leave family out of this chapter since we have a full chapter on that coming up.

The first example will be a friend. While in English, we don't say the word "friend" any differently, whether we are talking about a man or a woman. In French, there is a difference when writing the word, and therefore, a slight difference in pronunciation can be noticed. First, if you are talking about a male friend, you would call them *Un Ami* [uhn][ah-mee]. If you are talking about a female friend, you would say *Une Amie* [oo-nuh][ah-mee-uh]. Notice how the words are a little more drawn out to demonstrate the added *e*'s.

If you want to talk about your partner, you would say *mon petit ami* if you are talking about your boyfriend and *ma petite amie* if you are talking about your girlfriend. These translate to "my boyfriend" and "my girlfriend," respectively.

If you are talking about your teacher or your professor, you could say a few different things. The options are explained below:

Une/Un/La / Le Professeur(e)

Une/Un / L' Enseignant(e)

With these two options, either one can mean a teacher, and if you are talking about a university professor, you can use the first option. Both of these would be preceded by *Le* or *Un*, depending on if you want to say *a (un)* or *the (le)*. The second example drops the *e* from *le* because the word *enseignant* begins with a vowel. This is done for smooth speaking and to avoid a mouthful of vowels tripping you up. As you now know, adding *e* or *s* to the end is dependent on who you are speaking about. You will add an *e* for a female teacher or professor and an *s* for multiples.

The French word for "group" is very similar to the English word, though you will roll your tongue in the pronunciation, which is noted in the vocabulary list. In French, the word is *groupe*. Notice how, in this example, the word ends with the letter *e*? Since this one is not in brackets, it tells us that the *e* is a part of the word and not a letter that is added according to the gender of the person. The word for a club is also quite similar to the English word, except for the pronunciation. In French, we would say *Une Club* pronounced as, *[oon][k-loo-b]*. If you want to mention a team of some sort, you would say *l'Equipe* [ay-keep], which means the team.

Another person you may need to reference would include a coworker or a colleague, which, in French, is *un collègue*.

If you want to mention someone who is an acquaintance of yours, and you don't want to call them a friend or they are not a colleague, you would say *une connaissance*.

If there is someone who you do not like, you would say *un(e) ennemi(e)* when describing them, which means that they are "an enemy." If you want to say "my enemy," you would say *mon ennemi(e)*.

Now, we will look at a few sentence examples so that you can use these when speaking to someone:

Elle est une de mes ennemies. She is one of my enemies.

Il est sur l'équipe. He is on the team.

Il est mon collègue. He is my colleague.

Elle est ma professeure. She is my teacher/professor.

For any of the examples of people above, you can insert them into a sentence by saying one of the following:

Il/elle est le/la/une _____ de mon ami(e). She/he is the _____ of my friend.

il/elle est mon/ma _____. She/he is my _____.

With these examples, there are a few things to keep in mind. Notice the (e) at the end of *ami*. It is there because, depending on the gender of the friend about which you are speaking, you will either add the letter *e* to the end or not. Also, you see "le/la/une." Which of these you use will depend on the title you are using. For example, if you were saying, "She is a colleague of my friend," you would say *Elle est un collègue de mon ami*. However, if you were saying, "She is an enemy of my friend," you would say *Elle est une ennemie de mon ami*. Notice how these can vary depending on the word you are inserting to create the sentence, so when you learn a word like *professeur* (teacher), be sure to also learn that *un* or *le* goes with it instead of *une* or *la*. This will make remembering it much easier when you go to form a sentence.

Nationalities

We will now look at the nationalities of the world and how we can say them in French. You can then see how to insert these into sentences at the end of this section. To begin, though, the word continent is *un continent.*

North America

L'Amérique du nord

Nord-Américain

Un Américain, Une Américain(e)(s)

Un Canadien, Une canadien(e)(s)

Le Mexique

Un Mexicain, Une Mexicaine

Europe

L'Europe

Européen(e)(s)

Français(e)(s)

Italien / Italienne

Grec, grecque

Suisse

Belge

Suédois / Suédoise

Polonais

Islandais(e) / Icelandic

One example that is a little tricky is when we describe someone who is English. We would say they are *Anglais(e)*. However, when we speak about England as a country, we call it *L'Angleterre*.

Asia

L'Asie

Asiatique

Japonais(e)

Coréen(e)

Chinois(e)

Taïwanais(e)

South America

L'Amérique du sud

Sud-Américain(e)

Brésilien(ne)

Argentin(e), Argentinian

Africa

L' Afrique

Africain(e)

Sud-Africain

Kényan, Kenyan

Australia

L'Australie

L'Australien(e)

New Zetland

Néo-zélandais(e)

India

L'Inde

Indien(ne)

Antarctica

L'antarctique

Notice how these nationalities have the letter *e* and *s* in brackets at the end of them. What this means is that it depends on who you are speaking about. If you are speaking about a female, you will add the letter *e* to the end of the word. If you are speaking about multiple people, you will add the letter *s,* and if you are speaking about multiple women, you will add both. For example, "those Americans," if you are speaking about all women, would be *Les Americaines*. Notice how we have added both an *e* and an *s*. The reason that this is important to note in conversational French is that this will change the pronunciation slightly. You can see this in the vocabulary list at the end of this chapter.

We will now look at some practical examples of how to use these nationalities in a sentence.

Elle habite au continent de L'amérique du nord. Elle est Canadienne.

Il est *Coréen*

Elle est *Coréen*e

Occupations

Docteur [dok-t-ur], Doctor

Dentiste [don-tee-s-t], Dentist

Postier [poh-s-tee-ay], Mailman

Promeneur de Chien [p-roh-men-ur][duh][sh-yen], Dog Walker

Avocat [ah-vo-k-ah], Lawyer

Professeur [pro-f-ess-err], Teacher

Comptable [k-om-tah-b-luh], accountant

Conducteur de camion[k-on-doo-k-tur][duh][k-am-ee-on], truck driver

Banquier [bon-k-ee-yay], male banker

Banquière [bon-k-ee-y-air], female banker

Vocabulary List for Chapter 2

Connaître les gens, la nationalité et l'emploi

Knowing People

Un Ami [uhn][ah-mee], a friend

Une Amie [oo-n][ah-mee], a friend

Mon petit ami [m-oh][puh-tee][ah-mee], my boyfriend

Ma petite amie [m-ah][puh-tee-tuh][ah-mee], my girlfriend

Le Professeur(e) [luh][p-roh-f-ess-urr], the teacher

L' Enseignant(e) [l-on-sen-y-ohn-t], the teacher

Un Groupe [uhn][g-roo-puh], a group

Club [k-loo-b], club

Equipe [ay-keep], team

Un collègue [uhn][k-aw-l-egg], a colleague

Une connaissance [oo-n][k-on-ess-on-s], an acquaintance

Un ennemi [uhn][eh-n-eh-m-ee], an enemy

Une ennemie [oo-n][eh-n-eh-m-ee], an enemy

Mon ennemi [m-oh][eh-n-eh-m-ee], my enemy

Elle est une de mes ennemies [el][ay][oo-n][duh][m-eh][eh-n-eh-m-ee] She is one of my enemies.

Il est sur l'équipe [eel][ay][s-oo-r][l-eh-k-ee-puh]. He is on the team

Il est mon collègue [eel][ay][m-oh][k-aw-l-egg]. He is my colleague

Elle est ma professeure [el][ay][mah][pr-aw-f-ess-urr]. She is my teacher/professor.

Elle est un collègue de mon ami. [el][ay][uhn][k-aw-l-egg][duh][m-oh][ah-mee]. She is a colleague of my friend.

Elle est une ennemie de mon ami [el][ay][uhn][eh-n-eh-m-ee][duh][m-oh][ah-mee]. She is an enemy of my friend.

Nationalities

Un Continent [uhn][k-on-tee-n-on-t], a continent

L' Amérique du nord, [l-ah-meh-r-ee-k][doo][n-or], North America

Un American, [uhn][ah-meh-ree-k-ah-n], an American

Une Américaine [oo-n][ah-meh-ree-k-ah-nuh], an American

Un Canadian [uhn][k-ah-nah-d-ee-yeh-n], a Canadian

Une canadienne [oo-n][k-ah-nah-d-ee-yeh-nuh], a Canadian

Le Mexique [luh][m-eh-k-see-k], Mexico

Un Mexicain [uhn][m-eh-k-see-k-ah-n], a Mexican

Une Mexicaine [oo-n][m-eh-k-see-k-ah-n], a Mexican

L'Europe [l-oo-roh-puh], Europe

Européen [eu-roh-peh-en], European

Français [f-ron-s-ay], French

Italien [eh-tah-l-ee-en], Italian

Italienne [eh-tah-l-ee-en-uh], Italian

Grec [g-reh-k], Greek

Suisse [s-wee-suh], Swiss

Belge [b-el-j], Belgian

Suédois [s-weh-d-wah], Swedish

Suédoise [s-weh-d-wah-suh], Swedish

Polonais [poh-loh-nay], Polish

Anglais, [on-g-lay], English

L'Angleterre [l-on-g-let-air], England

Islandais [ee-lon-day], Icelandic

L'Asie [l-as-ee], Asia

Japonais [jah-poh-nay], Japanese

Coréen [k-oh-ray-en], Korean

Chinois [sh-ee-n-wah], Chinese

Taïwanais [t-eye-wah-n-ay], Taiwanese

L'Amérique du sud [l-ah-meh-ree-k][d-oo][s-oo-d], South America

Sud-Américain [s-oo-d][ah-meh-ree-k-an], South American

Brésilien [b-reh-see-lee-en], Brazilian

Brésilienne [b-reh-see-lee-en-nuh], Brazilian

Argentin [ar-j-on-t-eh-n], Argentinian

Argentine [ar-j-on-tee-nuh], Argentinian

L'Afrique [l-ah-f-ree-k], Africa

Africain [ah-f-ree-k-ah-n], African

Sud-Africain [s-oo-d][ah-f-ree-k-ah-n], South African

Kényan, [k-eh-n-yeh-n], Kenyan

L'Australie [l-aw-s-t-rah-lee], Australia

L'Australien [aw-s-t-rah-lee-en], Australian

Néo-zélandais [n-eh-oh][z-ay-lon-day], New Zealander

Néo-zélandaise [n-eh-oh][z-ay-lon-day-suh], New Zealander

L'Inde [l-eh-n-duh], India

Indien [l-eh-n-dee-en], Indian

Indienne [l-eh-n-dee-en-uh], Indian

L'antarctique [l-an-tar-k-tee-k], Antarctica

Islandais(e) [ee-l-on-day], Icelandic

Occupations

Docteur *[dok-t-ur], doctor*

Dentiste *[don-tee-s-t], dentist*

Postier *[poh-s-tee-ay], mailman*

Promeneur de Chien [p-roh-men-ur][duh][sh-yen], dog walker

Avocat [ah-vo-k-ah], lawyer

Professeur [pro-f-ess-err], teacher

Comptable [k-om-tah-b-luh], accountant

Conducteur de camion [k-on-doo-k-tur][duh][k-am-ee-on], truck driver

Banquier [bon-k-ee-yay], male banker

Banquière [bon-k-ee-y-air], female banker

Chapter 3: Family

La famille

In this chapter, we will look at the members of your family and how you can refer to them in French. Most of the time, when you are using these words, it will be when talking about someone to someone else, so we will also look at how to say this in a sentence and what words will need to come before and after them. To begin, below are the names for the different members of your family.

Père [p-air], Father

Mère [m-air], Mother

Soeur [s-urr], Sister

Frère [f-r-air], Brother

Cousine [k-oo-zee-n], Female Cousin

Cousin [k-oo-z-in], Male cousin

Tante [t-on-t], Aunt

Oncle [on-k-leh], Uncle

Grandmère [g-ron-d-m-air], Grandmother

Grandpère [g-ron-d-p-air], Grandfather

Grandparents, Grandparents

Demi-Soeur [duh-mee][s-urr], stepsister

Demi-Frère [duh-mee][f-r-air], stepbrother

Belle Frère [b-el][f-r-air], brother in law

Belle Soeur [b-el][s-urr], sister in law

Belle Mère [b-el][m-air], mother in law

We will now look at how to use these words in a sentence. These words will come in handy when you are talking to someone about someone else who is related to you, or if you are speaking within a family setting about other family members. Keep in mind that according to the gender of the person you are speaking about, you will need to change the word you use to describe them. In French, we have different ways of saying "my" according to gender. We will use *ma* if we are speaking about a female, like *my mother* or *my aunt*, and *mon* if we are speaking about a male, like *my father* or *my male cousin*. If you are using the plural, like *my cousins* or *my grandparents*, you will say *mes*, regardless of gender. Below are examples of this and how you can use them practically in a sentence.

Ma belle-soeur

Mon oncle

Ma tante

Mon cousin

Ma cousine

Some common sentences where you would use these words are to follow.

Le frère de ma mère est mon oncle. The brother of my mother is my uncle.

Le Petit Ami de ma soeur s'appelle Jean. My sister's boyfriend is named Jean.

Ma cousine est mon meilleur ami. My (female) cousin is my best friend.

Mon frère joue au baseball. My brother plays baseball.

Ma grand-mère est très belle. My grandmother is very pretty.

Je suis allez chez mes grand parents. I went to my grandparents' house.

J'ai mangé le petit déjeuner avec ma mère. I ate breakfast with my mother.

Mon père m'a conduit à l'école ce matin. My father drove me to school this morning.

As you learn more about the French language, you will be able to substitute any of these sentence examples with different nouns of your choice. For example, you could switch "school" to "hockey practice" or something of the sort. You can also switch out the person you are talking about. For example, instead of saying, "I went to my grandparent's house," you could say, "I went to my cousin's house." Knowing the basics of these types of sentences will allow you to create any type of sentence you want.

The above sentences concerned the family that you were born into, but now, we will look at other members of the family.

Ma femme, my wife

Mon mari, my husband

Une épouse, a spouse

Mes enfants, my kids

Mon fils, my son

Ma fille, my daughter

Un bébé, a baby

Un Bambin, a toddler

Les jumelles, twins

Now, we will use these in sentence examples for you to see how to use them practically.

J'adore ma femme. I love/adore my wife.

Avez-vous entendu que Jacques a maintenant une épouse? Have you heard that Jacques now has a spouse?

Les jumelles sont très enjouées! The twins are very playful!

Mes enfants sont âgés maintenant. My kids are grown now.

Vocabulary List for Chapter 3

When reading through this list, practice the pronunciation of these words, especially the first five, as you will see them over and over again in the example sentences further down the list. In the example sentences, the words that have not yet been spelled out for you to practice their pronunciation will be written between the brackets below the sentence itself and the words that you have practiced the pronunciation of can be found earlier in the list. Be sure to read aloud for the best results!

La famille

Ma [mah], my

Mon [m-oh], my

De [duh], of

La [l-ah], the

Le [luh], the

Père [p-air], father,

Mère [m-air], mother

Soeur [s-urr], sister

Frère [f-r-air], brother

Cousine [k-oo-zee-n], female cousin

Cousin [k-oo-z-in], male cousin

Tante [t-on-t], aunt

Oncle [on-k-leh], uncle

Grand-mère [g-ron-d-m-air], grandmother

Grand-père [g-ron-d-p-air], grandfather

Demi-Soeur [duh-mee][s-urr], stepsister

Demi-Frère [duh-mee][f-r-air], stepbrother

Belle Frère [b-el][f-r-air], brother in law

Belle Soeur [b-el][s-urr], sister in law

Belle Mère [b-el][m-air], mother in law

Le frère de ma mère est mon oncle. My mother's brother is my uncle.

Est [eh]

Le Petit Ami de ma soeur s'appelle Jean. My sister's boyfriend is named Jean.

S'appelle [s-ah-peh-luh]

Ma cousine est mon meilleur ami. My (female) cousin is my best friend.

Meilleur [may-ur]

Mon frère joue au baseball. My brother plays baseball.

Joue [j-oo]

Au [oh]

Baseball [bay-suh-bah-l]

Ma grand-mère est très belle. My grandmother is very pretty.

Très [t-r-ay](rolled r)

Belle [b-el]

Je suis allez chez mes grand parents. I went to my grandparents' house.

Suis [s-wee]

Allez [ah-lay]

Chez [sh-ay]

Mes [m-ay]

J'ai mangé le petit déjeuner avec ma mère. I ate breakfast with my mother.

Mangé [m-on-j-ay]

Petit déjeuner [puh-t-ee][day-j-uh-nay]

Avec [ah-veh-k]

Mon père m'a conduit à l'école ce matin. My father drove me to school this morning.

M'a [m-ah]

Conduit [k-on-d-wee]

L'école [l-eh-k-oh-l]

Ce [s-uh]

Matin [mah-t-ah-n]

Ma femme [f-emm], my wife

Mon mari [mah-ree], my husband

Une épouse [ay-poo-suh], a spouse

Mes enfants [on-f-on-t-s], my kids

Mon fils [f-ee-suh], my son

Ma fille [fee], my daughter

Un bébé [bay-bay], a baby

Un Bambin [bah-m-b-ah-n], a toddler

Les jumelles [j-oo-m-el], twins

J'adore ma femme. I love/adore my wife.

J'adore [j-ah-d-oh-r]

Avez-vous entendu que Jacques a maintenant une épouse? Have you heard that Jacques now has a spouse?

Avez-vous [ah-vay-v-oo]

Entendu [on-ton-doo]

Que [k-uh]

Jacques [j-ah-k]

Maintenant [meh-n-tuh-nah-n-t]

Les jumelles sont très enjouées! The twins are very playful!

Sont [soh-n]

Enjoués [on-j-oo-ay]

Mes enfants sont âgés maintenant. My kids are grown now.

Ages [ah-j-ay]

Chapter 4:
Time/Days/Months/Seasons
Heure/Jours/mois/saisons

In this chapter, we will examine the words we use in French to describe the time, the date, and the seasons. This will give you a foundation to be able to understand conversations pertaining to the date or time, as well as reading materials like newspapers that will mention dates, seasons, and years.

Time

The first thing we will look at in this section is time. In French, there are more names for things like seconds, minutes, and hours than in English. You will also need to have some understanding of numbers from 1 to 12 and how to say things like half an hour or 45 minutes. We will look at all this and more in this first section.

The following list demonstrates the words in French for the sections of time that we use like seconds and hours. Take some time to go over this and to practice your pronunciation.

Une Seconde [seh-k-on-d], second

Une Minute [mee-n-oo-t], minute

Une Heure [euh-ruh], hour

Un Jour [j-oo-r], day

Une Semaine [suh-m-en], week

Un Mois [m-wah], month

Une Année [ah-nay], year

Un Dizaine d'années [dee-z-en][d-ah-nay], ten years / tens of years

Une vingtaine d'années [van-ten][d-ah-nay], twenty years

When we talk about "the time" as we say in English, we would normally say something like, "what time is it?" or "what's the time." In French, we say *L'Heure [l-euh-ruh]*, which is the equivalent of "the time" in French. You may also see it written as *heure*, which is, essentially, "time" or "hour." Below, you can see how we would use this in a phrase or in a conversation.

C'est quoi l'heure? and *Quelle heure a-till?* both translate to *What is the time?* in English

À Quelle heure avez-vous été née? What time were you born?

Savez-vous À Quelle heure est-ce-qu'on quitte? Do you know what time we are leaving?

L'École commence à quelle heure? What time does school start?

Now, we will learn the numbers from 1 to 12, as we will use these when talking about time. First, we will learn the way that the hours are said in French, before moving on to more specific times. Note that "hour" is *heure*, which is used for 1, and the plural is "*heures*," which is used for 2 to 12.

1. Un
2. Deux
3. Trois
4. Quatre
5. Cinq
6. Six
7. Sept
8. Huit
9. Neuf
10. Dix
11. Onze
12. Douze

When we talk about hours in French, it is quite straightforward, as we say the number and then the word "hours." *Douze heures*, for example, literally translates to mean "twelve hours." There isn't really a word for "o'clock" like we have in English.

We will now look at how we say things like "fifteen minutes" or "half an hour" in French. This will involve a bit more knowledge about the numbers, but with practice, you will be using it seamlessly in no time.

_:15   *Quinze*

_:30   *Trente*

_:45   *Quarante Cinq*

When it comes to expressions like "a quarter past twelve," we would say this in French in the following ways:

_:30, *et demi*

7:15, seven fifteen, quarter past seven / *sept heures quinze, sept heures et quart*

7:30, seven thirty, half past seven / *sept heures trente, sept heures et demi*

7:45, seven forty-five, quarter to eight / *sept heures quarante-cinq, sept heures moins quart*

Now that you know these, you can say virtually any time that you see on the clock by substituting the hour and whichever of the three options above you need. These three options, along with all of the hours themselves, will give you enough information to understand and say almost any time without having to know how to say all of the numbers from one to sixty in French. Below are a few more terms concerning time.

In French, the 24-hour clock is used instead of the 12-hour clock that we use in North America. You can use either when speaking, and people will usually know what you mean, as long as you specify if it is AM or PM. It will, however, be helpful to know the numbers from 13 to 24 as well since a person speaking to you will likely use the 24-hour format when talking about time.

Avant-Midi, AM

Après-Midi, PM

Midi, noon

When talking about *1:00PM,* we would say in French, "*une heure de l'après- midi."* Here's an example using AM: *11:00 AM onze heure de le matin.*

While the correct term for AM is *avant-midi,* when we use this in conversation, we would say *de le matin* instead, which translates to "in the morning." The reason for this is that *avant-midi* translates to "before noon," and *apres-midi* translates to "afternoon." Therefore, another way to say AM is "in the morning."

13:00 or 1 PM *treize*
14:00 or 2 PM *quatorze*
15:00 or 3 PM *quinze*
16:00 or 4 PM *seize*
17:00 or 5 PM *dix-sept*
18:00 or 6 PM *dix-huit*
19:00 or 7 PM *dix-neuf*
20:00 or 8 PM *vingt*
21:00 or 9 PM *vingt et un*
22:00 or 10 PM *vingt deux*
23:00 or 11 PM *vingt trois*

Again, attach *"heures"* to the terms to tell time. We will look at some sentence examples now, so you can see how to use these times practically by answering the questions that we learned earlier in this section.

Question: *C'est quoi l'heure? What's the time?*
Answer: *C'est dix-heures dans le matin. It's 10 o'clock in the morning.*

Question: *Quelle heure a-till? What time is it?*
Answer: *Il est vingt-trois heures. It is 23:00 (11:00PM).*

Question: *Savez-vous À Quelle heure est-ce-qu'on quitte? Do you know at what time are we leaving?*
Answer: *On quitte dans trois heures, à cinq heures de l'après-midi. We are leaving in three hours, at 5 o'clock in the afternoon (5:00PM).*

Question: *À Quelle heure avez-vous été née? What time were you born?*
Answer: *Je suis née à six-heures et demi du matin. I was born at 6:30 in the morning.*

Question: *L'école commence à quelle heure? What time does school start?*
Answer: *L'école commence à neuf heures moins quart dans le matin. School starts at quarter to nine in the morning (8:45 AM).*

Answer 2:   *L'école commence à huit heures quarante-cinq dans le matin. School starts at eight forty-five in the morning.*

Days of the Week

In this section, we will learn the days of the week and how to use them in a sentence. First, practice reading the days of the week aloud, along with their pronunciation, a few times to get comfortable with them all.

Lundi [l-uh-n-dee], Monday

Mardi [mah-r-dee](rolled r), Tuesday

Mercredi [meh-k-re-dee](rolled r), Wednesday

Jeudi [j-uh-dee], Thursday

Vendredi [von-d-ruh-dee] (rolled r), Friday

Samedi [sah-m-dee], Saturday

Dimanche [dee-mon-sh], Sunday

When we use the days of the week in a sentence in French, they should not be capitalized. This is unlike English, where we would capitalize the days of the week, as they are considered names or titles. If you see it written and are wondering if the newspaper printing company made a mistake, it is not a mistake, just the French way!

Un Jour, a day

La Semaine, the week

Les jours de la semaine, the days of the week

Prochaine, next

Dernière, last

Chaque jour, every day

Hier, yesterday

Demain, tomorrow

Aujourd'hui, today

We will look at some example sentences for you to practice now:

Quel jour est-ce qu'on voit le film? What day do we see the movie?

J'ai travaillé 3 jours la semaine dernière. I worked 3 days last week.

C'est la fête d'anniversaire de mon fils le mardi prochaine. It's my son's birthday party next tuesday.

Il fait du ski chaque jour sauf lundi. He skis every day except Monday.

Je suis heureux chaque vendredi. I am happy whenever Friday comes.

Months of the Year

Les mois, months

Une année, a year

Un an, a year

In this chapter, we will look at the months of the year. These, similar to the days of the week, are not regarded as proper nouns, thus not capitalized. This is different from English as we would always capitalize names and titles like this.

January *le Janvier*

February *le février*

March *le mars*

April *l'avril*

May *le mai*

June *le juin*

July *le juillet*

August *l'août*

September *le septembre*

October, *l'octobre*

November, *le novembre*

December, *le décembre*

Practice saying the names of the months aloud a few times over, so you get comfortable with the pronunciation, and then we will look at them used in sentences below.

Mon anniversaire est dans le mois de juin. My birthday is in the month of June.

Ma fille a été née le 30 janvier. My daughter was born on January 30th.

Les mois entre novembre et mars sont très froid à l'état de New York. The months between November and March are very cold in the state of New York.

Il pleut beaucoup dans le mois d'avril. It rains a lot in the month of April.

Years

We will now look at the way that we say years in French. While it may be a little confusing if you are not too familiar with the way to say large numbers in French. In this section, I will teach you the main things you need to know when it comes to years so that you will be able to understand other people talking about years and reading something with dates, as well as when you want to mention the year in a conversation.

There are two words we use to say "year." Which word you use will depend on the number the year ends with. For all years that end with the number zero (0), you will use the word *l'an* [l-o-n]. This means *"the year."* For years ending in any number other than zero, you will use the term *l'année* [l-ah-nay], which also means *"the year."* If you forget and mix up these, don't fret; nobody will curse you for using the wrong form of the words *the year*. It is, however, good to know both forms so that if you hear them, you know what the person is saying.

L'année, the year

L'an, the year

In a conversation, we will often be talking about the year when something happened, the year when we will be doing something in the future, or the year when we were born. Therefore, the most common years we would be using belong in the 1800s, 1900s, and the 2000s. We will look at how you would say this group of years below.

The word *mille* means one thousand. You will use this in almost any year you are talking about. If you are talking about the future or present years, you will then say *deux mille,* which, as you now know, means "two thousand" (*deux*, as you learned earlier in this chapter, means *two*). The next most common numbers will be 900, which in French is *neuf cent* and 800, which in French is *huit cent*. This is something you also know already since you learned the names for 8 and 9 earlier. *Cent* means a hundred.

Mille, a thousand

Cent, a hundred

Now you know how to say the following years:

1000, mille

2000, deux mille

1800, mille huit cent

1900, mille neuf cent

2800 deux mille huit cent

2900 deux mille neuf cent

(These last two you wouldn't use too often, but they are numbers you could say now nonetheless.)

The next types of numbers you need to know are the multiples of 10, from 20 to 90. They are listed below, along with their pronunciations. Practice these ones before moving to the next section, where we will put all of your knowledge together.

20 (Twenty), in French is called vingt *[v-ain-t].*

30 (Thirty), in French is called trente *[t-ron-t] (with a rolled r)*

40 (Forty), in French is called quarante *[ka-ron-t] (with a rolled r)*

50 (Fifty), in French is called cinquante *[s-ain-k-ont]*

60 (Sixty), in French is called soixante *[s-wah-s-ont]*

70, (Seventy), in French is called soixante-dix, *[s-wah-s-ont] [dee-s]*

80, (Eighty), in French is called quatre-vingts, *[cat-ruh](rolled r)[v-ain-t]*

90, (Ninety), in French is called quatre-vingt-dix, *[cat-ruh](rolled r)[v-ain-t][dee-s]*

You now also know how to say all of the following years and more:

L'an 1990 Mille neuf cent quatre-vingt dix (which means one thousand, nine hundred ninety)

L'an 2020 Deux mille vingt

L'an 2030 Deux mille trente

Now, remember how, earlier in this chapter, you learned how to say the numbers from 1 to 10 and from 11 to 19? These will then help you to learn how to say the year in French. You will have to memorize how to say the numbers, though. At this point, it would be easy for you to say the following years:

2019 Deux mille dix-neuf

1880 Mille huit cent quatre-vingts

1902 Mille neuf cent deux

2001 Deux mille un

2010 Deux mille Dix

1965 Mille Neuf Cent soixante cinq

As a final note, when it comes to talking about years, there are two more words that we sometimes use when speaking about years. Those are the years A.D. and the years B.C. In French, we say *ap.JC* and *av.JC*, respectively. These shorthands refer to the eras "Before Jesus Christ" and "After Jesus Christ." In French, we say *apres Jesus-Christ* and *avant Jesus-Christ*. The pronunciations for these are below:

Apres, [ah-pray]

Avant [ah-vont]

Jesus-Christ, [j-ay-z-oo][k-r-ee](rolled r)

In practice, it would look like this:

200BC, 200 *av. JC, l'an Deux Cent avant Jesus-Christ*

Dates

Dates are the next logical step when you know how to talk about years and months. We will put that knowledge together in this section so that you are able to talk about dates with their years. When talking about a date, we will begin by saying, *le,* which means "the." This is similar to English as it looks like this:

Je suis née le. I was born on...

Il est né le. He was born on...

Tu es née le. You were born on...

Le 6 janvier 1920, The sixth of January, 1920

In French, we write the dates in the order shown above, with the number first, followed by the month and then the year, whereas, in English, we would say January 6, 1920.

Seasons

The seasons are our last stop in this chapter, and while they don't involve numbers like the rest of the concepts in this chapter, they are often included when talking about dates and months. The pronunciation for these can be found in the vocabulary list at the end of this chapter.

Le Printemps, Spring

L'été, Summer

L'automne, Fall / Autumn

L'hiver, Winter

Putting It All Together: Sentence Examples

We will now look at some sentences that will put all the knowledge you have gained from this chapter together.

J'aime beaucoup l'automne, contrairement à l'hiver. I like the autumn very much, unlike winter.

Le Noël se passe dans l'hiver. Christmas happens in winter.

J'aime les groupes de musique rock des ans mille neuf cent quatre-vingt jusqu'à l'année mille neuf cent quatre-vingt-cinq. I like rock music groups from the years 1980 to the year 1985.

Je suis née dans le printemps, sur mardi le trois mai, mille neuf cent quatre-vingt à dix heures du matin. I was born in the spring on Wednesday, May 3rd, 1980 at 10 o'clock in the morning.

Vocabulary List for Chapter 4

Heure/Jours/mois/saisons

Une Seconde [seh-k-on-d], second

Une Minute [mee-n-oo-t], minute

Une Heure [euh-ruh], hour

Un Jour [j-oo-r], day

Une Semaine [suh-m-en], week

Un Mois [m-wah], month

Une Année [ah-nay], year

Un Dizaine d'années [dee-z-en][d-ah-nay], ten years / tens of years

Une vingtaine d'années [van-ten][d-ah-nay], twenty years

Les mois de l'année, the months of the year

L'Heure [l-euh-ruh], the time

C'est quoi l'heure? What's the time?

C'est [s-ay]

Quoi [k-wah]

Quelle heure À-till? What time is it?

Quelle [k-el]

A-till [ah-tee-luh]

Savez-vous À Quelle heure est-ce-qu'on quitte? Do you know what time we are leaving?

Est-ce-qu'on [ess-suh-k-on]

Quitte [kee-tuh]

À Quelle heure avez-vous été né? What time were you born?

Avez-vous [ah-vay-voo]

Né [n-ay]

L'école commence à quelle heure? What time does school start?

L'école [l-ay-k-oh-luh]

1 AM   *Une [oo-n] heure [eh]*

2 AM   *Deux [duh] heures [eh]*

3 AM   *Trois [t-r-wah] heures [eh]*

4 AM   *Quatre [k-ah-t-ruh] heures [eh]*

5 AM   *Cinq [s-ah-n-k] heures [eh]*

6 AM   *Six [see-z] heures [eh]*

7 AM   *Sept [s-eh-t] heures [eh]*

8 AM   *Huit [wee-t] heures [eh]*

9 AM   *Neuf [n-uh-f] heures [eh]*

10 AM *Dix [d-ee-z] heures [eh]*

11 AM *Onze [oh-n-z] heures [eh]*

12 AM *Douze [doo-zuh] heures [eh]*

_:15   *Quinze [k-ah-n-z]*

_:30   *Trente [t-ron-tuh]*

_:45   Quarante Cinq [kah-ron-tuh][s-ah-n-k]

_:30   et demi [ay][duh-mee]

3:15, three fifteen, quarter past three

Trois heures quinze [t-r-wah][euh-ruh][k-ah-n-z], trois heures et quart [t-r-wah] [euh-ruh][eh][k-ar]

3:30, three thirty

Trois heures trente [t-r-wah][euh-ruh][t-ron-tuh], trois heures et demie [t-r-wah][euh-ruh][ay][duh-mee]

3:45, three forty-five, quarter to four

Trois heures quarante-cinq [t-r-wah][euh-ruh][kah-ron-tuh][s-ah-n-k], quatre heures moins quart [k-ah-t-ruh][euh-ruh][m-wah-n][k-ar]

Avant-Midi [ah-v-on][mee-dee], AM

Après-Midi [ah-p-r-eh][mee-dee], PM

Midi [mee-dee], noon

1:00PM. In English: "une heure de l'après- midi" [oo-n][euh-ruh][duh][l-ah-p-r-eh][mee-dee]

11:00 AM onze heure de le matin [oh-n-z][euh-ruh][duh][luh][mah-t-ah-n]

13:00 treize [t-r-ez](rolled r) heures

14:00 quatorze [cat-or-z] heures

15:00 quinze [k-an-z] heures

16:00 seize [s-ez] heures

17:00 dix-sept [dee-set] heures

18:00 dix-huit [dee-sweet] heures

19:00 dix-neuf [dee-s-nuf] heures

20:00 vingt [v-ain-t] heures

21:00 vingt et un [v-ain-t][eyy][uhhn] heures

22:00 vingt-deux [v-ain-t][duh] heures

23:00 vingt-trois [v-ain-t][t-r-wah] heures

24:00 vingt-quatre [v-ain-t][k-ah-t-ruh] heures

Question: C'est quoi l'heure? What's the time?

Quoi [k-wah]

Answer: C'est dix-heures dans le matin. It's 10:00 in the AM.

Dans [d-on]

Matin [mah-t-ahn]

Les Jours de la Semaine

Lundi [l-uh-n-dee], Monday

Mardi [mah-r-dee](rolled r), Tuesday

Mercredi [meh-k-re-dee](rolled r), Wednesday

Jeudi [j-uh-dee], Thursday

Vendredi [von-d-ruh-dee] (rolled r), Friday

Samedi [sah-m-dee], Saturday

Dimanche [dee-mon-sh], Sunday

Expressions temporelles

Un Jour [j-oo-ruh], a day

La Semaine [suh-meh-n], the week

Prochaine [p-roh-sh-eh-n], next

Dernière [d-air-nee-y-air], last

Chaque jour [sh-ah-k][j-oo-ruh], every day

Les jours de la semaine, week days

Hier [yee-air], yesterday

Demain [duh-mah-nuh], tomorrow

Aujourd'hui [oh-j-oo-r-d-wee], today

We will look at some example sentences for you to practice now.

Quel jour est-ce qu'on voit le film? What day do we see the movie?

Est-ce [eh-suh]

Qu'on [k-on]

Voit [v-wah]

Film [f-ee-l-muh]

J'ai travaillé 3 jours la semaine dernière. I worked for 3 days last week.

J'ai [j-eh]

Travaillé [t-rah-v-I-yay]

C'est la fête d'anniversaire de mon fils le mardi prochaine. It's my son's birthday party next tuesday.

Fête [f-eh-tuh]

D'anniversaire [d-ah-nee-v-air-seh-ruh]

Il fait du ski chaque jour sauf lundi. He skis every day except Monday.

Il [eel]

Ski [s-k-ee]

Sauf [s-oh-fuh]

Je suis heureux chaque vendredi. I am happy whenever Friday comes.

Je suis [j-uh][s-wee]

Heureux [euh-r-uh]

January le janvier, [luh][j-on-vee-ay]

February le février, [luh][fay-v-ree-ay]

March le mars [luh][mah-r-se]

April l'avril, [l-ah-v-ree-l]

May le mai, [luh][may]

June le juin, [luh][j-wah-n]

July le juillet [luh][j-wee-ay]

August l'août [luh][oot]

September le septembre, [luh][sep-tom-b-ruh]

October, l'octobre, [l-oct-oh-b-ruh]

November, le novembre, [luh][no-vom-b-ruh]

December, le décembre, [luh][day-som-b-ruh]

Les mois entre novembre et mars sont très froid à l'état de New York. The months between November and March are very cold in the state of New York.

Entre [on-t-ruh]

Froid [f-r-wah]

L'état [l-eh-tah-t]

Il pleut beaucoup dans le mois d'avril. It rains a lot in the month of April.

Pleut [p-luh]

Beaucoup [boh-k-oo]

L'année, the year

L'an, the year

Mille [mee-luh], thousand

Cent [s-on-t], hundred

1000, mille

2000, deux mille [duh][mee-luh]

1800, mille huit cent [mee-luh][w-ee-tuh][s-on-t]

1900, mille neuf cent [mee-luh][n-uh-f][s-on-t]

2800 deux mille huit cent [duh][mee-luh][wee-tuh][s-on-t]

2900 deux mille neuf cent [duh][mee-luh][n-uh-f][s-on-t]

20 (Twenty), in French, it's called vingt [v-ain-t].

30 (Thirty), in French, it's called trente [t-ron-t] (with a rolled r)

40 (Forty), in French, it's called quarante [ka-ron-t] (with a rolled r)

50 (Fifty), in French, it's called cinquante [s-ain-k-ont]

60 (Sixty), in French, it's called soixante [s-wah-s-ont]

70, Seventy, in French, it's called soixante-dix, [s-wah-s-ont][dee-s]

80, Eighty, in French, it's called quatre-vingts, [cat-ruh](rolled r)[v-ain-t]

90, Ninety, in French, it's called quatre-vingt-dix, [cat-ruh](rolled r)[v-ain-t][dee-s]

1990 Mille neuf cent quatre-vingt-dix [mee-luh][n-uh-f][s-on-t][cat-ruh](rolled r)[v-ain-t][dee-s]

2020 Deux mille vingt [duh][mee-luh][v-ain-t]

2030 Deux mille trente [duh][mee-luh][t-ron-t] (with a rolled r)

2019 Deux mille dix-neuf [duh][mee-luh][d-ee-z][n-uh-f]

1880 Mille huit cent quatre-vingts [mee-luh][wee-t][s-on-t][cat-ruh](rolled r)[v-ain-t]

1902 Mille neuf cent deux [mee-luh][n-uh-f][s-on-t][duh]

2001 Deux mille un [duh][mee-luh][uh-n]

2010 Deux mille Dix [duh][mee-luh][d-ee-z]

1965 Mille Neuf Cent soixante cinq [mee-luh][n-uh-f][s-on-t][s-wah-s-ont][s-ah-n-k]

Apres, [ah-pray]

Avant [ah-vont]

Jésus-Christ, [j-ay-z-oo][k-r-ee](rolled r)

200BC, 200 av. JC, l'an Deux Cent avant Jésus-Christ [l-ah-n][duh][s-on-t][ah-v-on][j-ay-z-oo][k-r-ee](rolled r)

Je suis née le... I was born on...

Je [j-uh]

Suis [s-wee]

Née [n-ay]

Le [luh]

Il est né le... He was born on...

Est [ay]

Tu es née le... You were born on...

Es [ay]

Le Printemps [luh][p-r-ah-n-t-om-puh], Spring

L'été [l-ay-t-ay], Summer

L'automne [l-oh-t-oh-nuh], Fall / Autumn

L'hiver [l-ee-v-air], Winter

J'aime beaucoup l'automne, contrairement à l'hiver. I like the autumn very much, unlike winter.

J'aime [j-eh-muh]

Le Noël se passe dans l'hiver. Christmas happens in the winter.

Noel [n-oh-el]

Passe [pah-suh]

J'aime les groupes de musique rock des ans mille neuf cent quatre-vingt jusqu'à l'année mille neuf cent quatre-vingt-cinq. I like rock music groups from the years 1980 to the year 1985.

J'aime [j-eh-muh]

Groupes [g-r-oo-puh]

Musique [m-oo-z-ee-k]

Chapter 5: Weather

Météo

In this chapter, we will look at the terms we use in French to describe the weather and everything that goes with this. You will also learn how to use these terms in a sentence and the common phrases you would need to know when it comes to weather.

To begin, the word for "weather" itself is, *le temps*. You would use this word when talking about the weather in general as a topic.

If someone were to ask you about the weather, or you wanted to know how good or bad is the weather that day, you would use the question, *Quel temps fait-il?* This directly translates to "*What weather is it doing?*" The answer to this will be something that begins with the phrase "it is doing…" in French. Now, this may seem like an odd way to put it, but in French, this is how it is done, and this makes the most sense. If you ever forget how to answer a question about the weather, the clue is in their question, as you repeat the end of the phrase in your answer. Below are some examples of the answers you would hear or give when asked about the weather.

Il fait _____ degrés, It is _____ degrees.

Il fait chaud. It is hot (weather).

Il fait orageux. It is stormy.

Il fait humide. It is humid.

Il fait frais. It is cool (weather).

Il fait nuageux. It is cloudy.

Il fait froid. It is cold (weather).

Depending on the way the person asks you about the weather, if you are going to give a general response like, "it is nice outside" or "the weather is bad today," there are two different ways that you can say this. The first follows the pattern we have learned above, which begins with *il fait...* For this, you could use the sentence, *Il fait mauvais*, which translates to *it's bad outside*. *Il fait beau* translates to "It is nice outside." These directly translate to mean "it's doing bad" and "it's doing nice." You would use these in response to the question of "what weather is it doing? You can also respond to this by using *des intemperies,* which is a single word that means bad weather, and *Le beau temps,* which means good weather. These would be used in a sentence rather than as a response to the question *quel temps fait-il?* Two examples of these used in a sentence are below.

Il y a les dégâts dus aux intempéries. There is damage due to the bad weather.

Apres la tempête, on a reçu le beau temps! After the thunderstorm, we received good weather!

There are also other terms for more specific weather occurrences that you can use to describe what it is like outside. These are below.

Le foudre. In English, this means *lightning*

Le tonnerre. In English, this means *thunder*

Un coup de foudre. In English, this means *a bolt of lightning*

Un coup de tonnerre. In English, this means *a clash of thunder*

Cela tonnait. In English, this means *"It was thundering."*

Une inondation. In English, this means *a flood*

Une rafale. In English, this means *a gust of wind*

La grêle. In English, this means *hail*

We will look at the above terms used in sentences so that you can get a better idea of how to use them practically.

Hier, j'ai vu le foudre. Yesterday, I saw lightning

J'entends le tonnerre. I hear thunder

Mon père a dit qu'il a entendu un coup de tonnerre, et ma mère a vu un coup de foudre! My father said he heard a clap of thunder, and my mother saw a bolt of lightning.

Cela tonnait pendant les trois derniers jours. It was thundering for the past three days.

Je pense qu'une inondation vient. I think a flood is coming.

J'ai fermé la fenêtre parce qu'il y avait une rafale très grand. I closed the window because there was a very large gust of wind.

On doit rentrer chez nous car la grêle commence à tomber. We must go home because the hail begins to fall.

We will now look at some other weather-related descriptions, but these ones are slightly longer and are more phrases than single words. Notice how these ones begin with the word *c'est*. This word means "it is" or "it's" in French.

C'est un vague de froid. In English, it means, *It is a cold spell*

C'est un cyclone. In English, it means, *It is a cyclone.*

C'est un deluge. In English, it means, *It is a torrential downpour.*

C'est une giboulée. In English, it means, *It is a sudden rainstorm.*

C'est la canicule. In English, it means, *It is a heat wave.*

C'est un ouragan. In English, it means, *It is a hurricane.*

C'est un ouragan de catégorie _____. In English, it means, *It is a category ____ hurricane.*

C'est un orage. In English, it means, *It is a storm.*

C'est une tempête. In English, it means, *It is a thunderstorm.*

C'est une tornade. In English, it means, *It is a tornado.*

C'est un orage tropical. In English, it means, *It is a tropical storm.*

C'est un typhon. In English, it means, *It is a typhoon.*

We will look at these words used in sentence examples below:

C'est un ouragan de catégorie cinq, alors on doit quitter la ville. It's a category five hurricane, so we have to leave the town.

La pratique de soccer est annulée car un orage vient. Soccer practice is cancelled because a storm is coming.

Je ne veux pas aller au Mexique parce qu'un orage tropicale est prédit. I don't want to go to Mexico because a tropical storm is predicted.

Je ne veux pas faire du ski aujourd'hui car il y a un vague de froid. I don't want to ski today because there is a cold spell.

When speaking about the weather in terms of the forecast and the forecasting of weather, we use the word *la météo / la météorologie,* instead of *le temps.* This means "the weather forecast." Similarly, ths is what we call a weather chart, which is *une carte météorologique.*

Vocabulary List for Chapter 5

Météo

Le temps. [luh][tom-puh]

Quel temps fait-il? [k-el][tom-puh][f-ay-tuh][eel]

Il fait _____ degrés. It is _____ degrees.
[eel][f-ay] ___ [day-g-ray]

Il fait chaud. It's hot.
Chaud [sh-oh-d]

Il fait frais. In English, it means, *It is cool.*
Frais [f-ray]

Il fait froid. In English, it means, *It is cold.*
Froid [f-r-wah]

Il fait humide. It's humid.
Humide [h-oo-mee-duh]

Il fait nuageux. It's cloudy.
Nuageux [n-oo-ah-j-uh]

Il fait orageux. It's stormy.
Orageux [or-ah-j-uh]

Il fait mauvais. It's bad.

Mauvais [m-oh-v-ay]

Il fait beau. It's nice out.

Beau [b-oh]

Des intempéries

Intempéries [ah-n-tom-p-air-ee]

Le beau temps

[b-oh][tom-puh]

Il y a les dégâts dus aux intempéries. There is damage due to bad weather.

Il y a [ee-l-yee-ah]

Dégâts [day-g-ah]

Dus [doo]

Aux [oh]

Après la tempête, on a reçu le beau temps! After the thunderstorm, we received good weather!

Reçu [ray-s-oo]

Le foudre [f-oo-d-ruh], lightning

Le tonnerre [toh-n-air], thunder

Un coup [k-oo] de foudre [f-oo-d-ruh], a bolt of lightning

Un coup [k-oo] de tonnerre [toh-n-air], a clap of thunder

Cela tonnait [s-eh-lah][toh-nay], it was thundering

Une inondation [oo-n][eh-noh-n-d-ah-see-oh-n], a flood

Une rafale [r-ah-f-ah-luh], A gust of wind

La grêle [g-r-eh-luh], hail

Hier, j'ai vu le foudre. Yesterday, I saw lightning

Hier [yee-air]

J'entends le tonnerre. I hear thunder.

J'entends [j-on-t-on-d]

Mon père a dit qu'il a entendu un coup de tonnerre, et ma mère a vu un coup de foudre! My father said he heard a clap of thunder, and my mother saw a bolt of lightning.

Qu'il [k-eel]

Vu [v-oo]

Cela tonnait pendant les trois derniers jours. It was thundering for the past three days.

Pendant [p-on-d-on]

Je pense qu'une inondation vient. I think a flood is coming.

Pense [p-on-suh]

Vient [v-ee-yen]

J'ai fermé la fenêtre parce qu'il y avait une rafale très grand. I closed the window because there was a very large gust of wind.

Ferme [f-air-may]

Fenêtre [f-eh-n-eh-t-ruh]

Avait [ah-v-ay]

Grand [g-ron]

On doit rentrer chez nous car la grêle commence à tomber.

Rentrer [ron-t-ray]

Chez [sh-ay]

Nous [n-oo]

Car [k-ar]

C'est [say]

C'est un vague de froid. It's a cold spell.

Vague [v-ah-g-uh]

C'est un cyclone [see-k-l-oh-nuh]. In English, it means, It is a cyclone.

C'est un déluge [day-l-oo-j]. In English, it means, It is a torrential downpour.

C'est une giboulée [g-ee-boo-lay]. In English, it means, It is a sudden rainstorm.

C'est la canicule [k-ah-nee-k-oo-l]. In English, it means, It is a heat wave.

C'est un ouragan [oo-rah-g-on]. In English, it means, It is a hurricane.

C'est un ouragan de catégorie [k-ah-t-eh-g-oh-ree] _____. In English, it means, *It is a category _____ hurricane.*

C'est un orage [oh-rah-j]. In English, it means, *It is a storm.*

C'est une tempête [tom-p-eh-tuh]. In English, it means, *It is a thunderstorm.*

C'est une tornade [t-or-nah-duh]. In English, it means, *It is a tornado.*

C'est un orage tropical [t-roh-p-ee-k-ah-luh]. In English, it means, *It is a tropical storm.*

C'est un typhon [tee-f-on], In English, it means, *It is a typhoon.*

La pratique de soccer est annulée car un orage vient. Soccer practice is cancelled because a storm is coming.

Pratique [p-rah-tee-kuh]

Soccer [s-oh-k-air]

Annulée [ah-n-oo-lay]

Car [k-ar]

Je ne veux pas aller au Mexique parce qu'un orage tropicale est prédit. I don't want to go to Mexico because a tropical storm is predicted.

Mexique [m-ex-ee-k]

Prédit [p-ray-d-ee]

Je ne veux pas faire du ski aujourd'hui car il y a un vague de froid. I don't want to ski today because there is a cold spell.

Faire [f-air]

Aujourd'hui [oh-j-oo-r-d-wee]

Une carte météorologique [k-ar-t][may-tay-oh-roh-loh-j-ee-k], a weather chart

La météo [may-tay-oh] / la météorologie, the weather forecast

Chapter 6: Food

La Nourriture

In this chapter, we will look at everything related to food. We will look at how to go through the entire process in a restaurant: from walking in to leaving, including ordering food and asking for anything you may need. We will look at some common foods and how to say them in French, as well as things like grocery shopping and fast food. At the end of each food section located within this chapter, you will find sentence examples for how you can use these words in a sentence. This will also show you what other words are commonly used in conjunction with common food words. At the end of the chapter is a vocabulary list where you can find all the pronunciations for the words in this chapter.

First, we will look at the words we use for food.

La nourriture, food

Manger, to eat

Un repas, a meal

Avoir Faim, to be hungry

La cuisine, the kitchen

Le Petit Déjeuner, breakfast

Le déjeuner, lunch

Le diner, dinner

Diner, to have dinner

Le goûter, snack

Goûter, to taste

Bon Appétit, enjoy your food / let's eat

Groceries, *Épicerie*

When it comes to groceries, you may need to know how to ask for things when you go to the store. You may also need to know what the most common foods are called in French for conversation's sake. In this section, we will look at these.

Staples, *Agrafes*

Staples are those things that we keep in the house all the time and come in handy, no matter what we are making. Below, you will find these, along with their names in French.

La farine, flour

Les oeufs, eggs

Le beurre, butter

L'huile d'olive, olive oil

Du lait, milk

Le pain, bread

Le sucre, sugar

Le fromage, cheese

J'aime manger le fromage avant- le dîner. I like eating cheese before dinner.

Les Oeufs sur le pain est mon petit déjeuner préféré. Eggs on toast is my favorite breakfast.

Je mis du sucre dans mon Café. I put sugar in my coffee.

Vegetables and Fruits

Now, we will look at the names for the most common vegetables and fruits in French. Their pronunciation can be found in the vocabulary list at the end of the chapter.

Les légumes, vegetables

Les asperges, asparagus

La carotte, a carrot

Les champignons, mushrooms

La pomme de terre, a potato

La laitue, lettuce

Un oignon, an onion

Le maïs, corn

Le concombre, a cucumber

Les épinards, spinach

La tomate, a tomato

Les fruits, fruits

Une banane, a banana

Un fruit de la passion, a passion fruit

Un ananas, a pineapple

Les cerises, cherries

Une fraise, a strawberry

Une goyave, a guava

Une orange, an orange

Un pomélo, a pomelo

Une pomme, an apple

Une grappe de raisin, a bunch of grapes

J'adore les légumes verts comme le concombre, les asperges et la laitue. I love green vegetables like cucumbers, asparagus, and lettuce.

Je ne sais pas si une tomate est un fruit ou un végétale. I don't know if a tomato is a fruit or a vegetable.

Les raisins forment le vin après quelques processus. Grapes make wine after some processes.

Meat

The words in this section describe foods related to or containing meat.

La viande, meat

Le poulet, chicken

La dinde, turkey

De boeuf, beef

Le jambon, ham

Le bifteck, steak

Le poisson, fish

Le porc, pork

Le saucisson, sausage

Le blanc de poulet. In English, this translates to *the chicken breast*

Le coquelet. In English, this means *young, male chicken*

Le poulet/poule. This also translates to *chicken*

Le poulet rôti. In English, this means *roast chicken*

La volaille. In English, this translates to *the white meat*

Le consommé de la volaille. In English, this translates to *chicken broth*

La cuisse. In English, this means *dark meat*

La poularde. In English, this translates to *young, female chicken*

Les ailes de poulet. In English, this translates to *the chicken wings*

Les végétariens ne mangent pas la viande.

Les végétaliens ne mangent ni viande, ni œufs ni rien de semblable. Vegans don't eat meat or eggs or any of the sort.

J'aime manger le poulet mais seulement la volaille et pas la cuisse. I like eating chicken but only white meat and not dark meat.

Others/Dishes, *Autres/plats*

Les pâtes, pasta

Le riz, rice

Le chocolat, chocolate

Le gâteau, cake

La tarte, pie

La confiture, jam

La confiture sur du pain est un bon casse-croûte. Jam on bread is a good snack.

On mange le gâteau chaque fois qu'on a une fête d'anniversaire. We eat cake every time we have a birthday party.

Qu'est-ce que tu aimes de plus, les pâtes ou le riz? Which do you like better, pasta or rice?

Fast-Food

In French, fast food is called *Le restauration rapide*. This means exactly the same as in English. The most common fast food words are found in this section.

Les frites, French fries

Un Hamburger, a hamburger

Le hot dog

La boisson non-alcoolisée, a pop

La pizza, pizza

La garniture, the filling

Les beignets de poulet, In English means, *chicken nuggets*

Le poulet frit, fried chicken

Le poisson avec des frites, In English means, *fish and chips*

Le soda, soda pop

À emporter, to take-out

Le plateau, a tray

La paille, a straw

La sauce, sauce

Le poulet frit avec de la sauce piquante s'il vous plaît. Fried chicken with hot sauce, please.

J'ai oublié une paille pour mon soda! I forgot a straw for my soda!

Je voudrais un hamburger avec du fromage et de la laitue. I would like a hamburger with cheese and lettuce.

Putting It All Together: Sentence Examples

In this final section, we will look at sentence examples that use a bunch of these terms, as well as some others you may have learned so far in this book. This is because the likelihood that you will see or use any of these words alone is slim, and knowing how to put them together with other words will be the key to your success in speaking and understanding the language.

Pour l'action de grâces, on mange de la dinde, les patates, les carottes, les asperges et pour le dessert on mange de la tarte. For thanksgiving, we are eating turkey, potatoes, carrots, asparagus, and for dessert, we are eating pie.

Sur mon pizza, j'aime avoir de poulet, les ananas, les épinards et du fromage suisse. Avant que je le mange, je mis des sauces piquantes au-dessus aussi. On my pizza, I like to have chicken, pineapple, spinach, and Swiss cheese. Before I eat it, I put hot sauce on top, as well.

Quand je commande un bifteck, je veux que le cuisinier le cuit jusqu'au point qu'il est mi-saignant. When I order a steak, I want the chef to cook it to the point that it is medium rare.

Vocabulary List for Chapter 6

La Nourriture

La nourriture [noo-ree-too-ruh], food

Manger [mon-j-ay], to eat

Le repas [ray-pah], a meal

Avoir Faim [ah-v-wah-ruh][f-ah-m], to be hungry

La cuisine [lah][k-wee-zee-nuh], the kitchen

Le Petit Déjeuner [puh-tee][day-j-uh-nay], breakfast

Le déjeuner [day-j-uh-nay], lunch

Le dîner [dee-nay], dinner

Dîner [dee-nay], to have dinner

Le goûter [g-oo-tay], snack

Goûter [g-oo-tay], to taste

Bon Appétit [b-oh-n][ah-puh-tee], enjoy your food / let's eat

Les oeufs [uh-f], eggs

Le pain [p-ah-nuh], bread

Le beurre [b-uh-r], butter

Du lait [lay], milk

La farine [f-ah-ree-nuh], flour

L'huile d'olive [l-wee-luh][d-oh-lee-vuh], In English, this means "the olive oil"

Le sucre [s-oo-k-ruh], sugar

Le fromage [f-roh-mah-j], cheese

J'aime manger le fromage avant- le dîner. I like eating cheese before dinner.

Avant [ah-v-on]

Les Oeufs sur le pain est mon petit déjeuner préféré. Eggs on toast is my favorite breakfast.

Sur [s-oo-r]

Préféré [p-ray-f-air-ay]

Je mis du sucre dans mon Café. I put sugar in my coffee.

Mis [mee]

Dans [d-on]

Les légumes [l-ay-g-oo-m], vegetables

Les asperges [ah-s-p-air-j], asparagus

La carotte [k-ah-r-oh-tuh], a carrot

Les champignons [sh-om-p-ee-n-y-on], mushrooms

Le concombre [k-on-k-om-b-ruh], a cucumber

La laitue [lay-too], lettuce

Un oignon [oh-nee-oh], an onion

La pomme de terre [p-oh-m][duh][t-air], a potato

Le mais [m-ah-yee-suh], corn

La tomate [toh-mah-tuh], a tomato

Les fruits [f-r-wee], fruits

Un ananas [ah-nah-nah], a pineapple

Une banane [bah-nah-nuh, a banana

Une fraise [f-r-eh-z], a strawberry

Les cerises [s-air-ee-z], cherries

Une orange [oh-ron-j], an orange

Une pomme [p-oh-m], an apple

Un raisin [ray-z-ah-nuh], a grape

J'adore les légumes verts comme le concombre, les asperges et la laitue. I love green vegetables like cucumbers, asparagus, and lettuce.

J'adore [j-ah-d-oh-ruh]

Vert [v-air]

Comme [k-uh-m]

Je ne sais pas si une tomate est un fruit ou un végétale. I don't know if a tomato is a fruit or a vegetable.

Sais [s-ay]

Si [see]

Ou [oo]

Les raisins forment le vin après quelques processus. Grapes make wine after some processes.

Forment [f-oh-r-m-uh]

Vin [v-ah-n]

Après [ah-p-ray]

Quelques [k-el-k-uh]

Processus [p-r-aw-s-ess-oo]

La viande [vee-on-duh], meat

Le poulet [p-oo-lay], chicken

Le blanc [b-l-on-k] de poulet, chicken breast

La dinde [d-ah-n-d], turkey

La volaille [v-ol-eye], white meat

De boeuf [b-uh-f], beef

Le jambon [j-ah-m-b-oh-n], ham

Le coquelet [k-oh-k-lay], young male chicken

Le bifteck [b-if-t-eh-k], steak

Le poisson [p-wah-s-on], fish

Le porc [p-oh-r-k], pork

Le saucisson [s-oh-see-s-on], sausage

Le consommé de la volaille [k-on-s-om-ay][d-oo][v-ol-eye], chicken broth

La cuisse [k-wee-s], dark meat

La poularde [p-oo-l-ar], young female chicken

Le poulet rôti [r-oh-tee], roast chicken

Les ailes [eye] de poulet, chicken wings

Les végétariens ne mangent pas la viande.

Végétariens [v-ay-j-ay-tah-ree-en]

Les végétaliens ne mangent ni viande, ni œufs ni rien de semblable. Vegans don't eat meat or eggs or any of the sort.

Végétaliens [v-ay-j-ay-tah-lee-en]

Ni [nee]

J'aime manger le poulet mais seulement la volaille et pas la cuisse. I like eating chicken but only white meat and not dark meat.

Seulement [s-uh-l-mon]

Pas [pah]

Les pâtes [pah-tuh], pasta

Le riz [r-ee], rice

Le chocolat [sh-oh-k-oh-lah], chocolate

Le gâteau [g-ah-t-oh], cake

La tarte [t-art], pie

La confiture [k-on-fee-too-ruh], jam

La confiture sur du pain est un bon casse-croûte. Jam on bread is a good snack.

Bonne [boh-nuh]

Casse-croute [k-ass][k-roo-tuh]

On mange le gâteau chaque fois qu'on a une fête d'anniversaire. We eat cake every time we have a birthday party.

Chaque [sh-ah-k]

Fois [f-wah]

Fête [f-eh-tuh]

D'anniversaire [d-ah-nee-v-air-s-air]

Qu'est-ce que tu aimes le plus, les pâtes ou le riz? Which do you like better, pasta or rice?

Aime [em]

Ou [oo]

Le restauration rapide [r-es-toh-r-ah-see-on][rah-pee-duh], fast food

Les frites [f-ree-tuh], French fries

Un Hamburger [om-b-eh-r-g-ur], a hamburger

Le hot dog [oh-t][d-og], hot dog

La boisson non-alcoolisée [b-wah-s-on][non][al-k-oh-ol-ee-say], a pop

La pizza [p-ee-z-ah], pizza

La garniture [g-ar-nee-too-ruh], the filling

La sauce [s-oh-s], sauce

Les beignets de poulet [ben-yet][duh][p-oo-lay], chicken nuggets

Le poulet frit [f-ree], fried chicken

Le poisson avec des frites, fish and chips

[luh][p-wah-son][ah-ve-k][d-ay][f-ree-tuh]

A emporter [om-por-tay], to take-out

Le plateau [p-lah-toh], a tray

La paille [pah-y], a straw

Le poulet frit avec de la sauce piquante s'il vous plaît. Fried chicken with hot sauce, please.

Avec [ah-ve-k]

Piquante [pee-k-on-t-uh]

J'ai oublié une paille pour mon soda! I forgot a straw for my soda!

Oublie [oo-b-lee-ay]

Je voudrais un hamburger avec du fromage et de la laitue. I would like a hamburger with cheese and lettuce.

Voudrais [voo-d-ray]

Pour l'action de grâces, on mange de la dinde, les patates, les carottes, les asperges et pour le dessert on mange de la tarte. For thanksgiving, we are eating turkey, potatoes, carrots, asparagus, and for dessert, we are eating pie.

L'action de grâces [l-ah-k-see-on][duh][g-rah-suh]

Sur mon pizza, j'aime avoir de poulet, les ananas, les épinards et du fromage suisse. Avant que je le mange, je mis des sauces piquantes au-dessus aussi. On my pizza, I like to have chicken, pineapple, spinach, and Swiss cheese. Before I eat it, I put hot sauce on top, as well.

Sur [soo-ruh]

Quand je commande un bifteck, je veux que le cuisinier le cuit jusqu'au point qu'il est mi-saignant. When I order a steak, I want the chef to cook it to the point that it is medium rare.

Quand [k-on-d]

Veux [v-uh]

Cuisinier [k-wee-see-nee-ay]

Cuit [k-wee]

Point [p-wah-n-t]

Mi-saignant [mee][s-ah-g-non-t]

Chapter 7: Home

In this chapter, we will look at the terms concerning the home. This will get you ready to go shopping for homeware, have conversations about your home, and ask people questions about their homes when you visit them. To begin, we will look at the house in general, and then we will examine the house room-by-room.

La maison, the house/the home

Un appartement, an apartment

Le sous-sol, the basement

Les escaliers, the stairs

Le toit, the roof

La fenêtre, the window

La porte, the door

La table, the table

Les rideaux, the curtains

Un tapis, a carpet / a rug

Le plafond, the ceiling

Le mur, the wall

L'arrière-cour, the backyard

Le porche, the porch

La boîte aux lettres, the mailbox

Le pont, the deck

Ma maison est très réconfortante après une longue journée. My house is very comforting/soothing after a long day.

Mon mari a acheté la table et le tapis hier soir. My husband bought the table and the carpet yesterday night.

Je construis le pont avec mon fils. I am building the deck with my son.

Now, we will look at each room in the house and what you would find in each room and how to say these things in French. We will then look at how to use them in a sentence.

The Kitchen

La cuisine, the kitchen

Un couteau, a knife

Un four, an oven

Une fourchette, a fork

Une cuillère, a spoon

Une chaise, a chair

La table à manger, the dining table

Le réfrigérateur, the refrigerator

Le frigo, the fridge (this term is more of a slang word)

Je vais à la cuisine pour manger. I am going to the kitchen to eat.

J'aime manger la soupe avec une cuillère. I like eating soup with a spoon.

Je vais faire une tarte dans le four. I am going to make a pie in the oven.

The Bedroom

La chambre, the bedroom

Une armoire, a closet

Un lit, a bed

Un oreiller, a pillow

Un couvercle, a comforter

Le tapis, the carpet

La commode, the dresser

Je veux lire dans mon lit. I like reading in my bed.

J'aime mon nouveau couvercle avec les cercles bleus. I like my new comforter with blue circles.

Je mis mes vêtements dans la commode. I put my clothes in the dresser.

The Bathroom

La salle de bain, the bathroom

La toilette, the toilet

Le lavabo, the sink

La baignoire, the bathtub

Le miroir, the mirror

La douche, the shower

L'armoire de toilette, the bathroom cabinet

Je vais laver mes mains dans le lavabo. I'm going to wash my hands in the sink.

Je me détends dans la baignoire. I relax / unwind in the bathtub.

Je dois aller à la toilette. In English, it means I have to go to the toilet.

The Living Room

La salle de séjour, the living room

Le sofa, the couch

Le fauteuil, the armchair

La télévision, the television

La table basse, coffee table

Les jeux de société, board games

L'ordinateur, the computer

Le bureau, the desk

La console de jeu, the game system

Je fais mon travail de l'école au bureau. I do my school work at the desk.

Je joue les jeux de société avec mon père et mon frère chaque lundi soir. I play board games with my father and my brother every Monday night.

Dans le fauteuil vert, c'est mon place préférée pour regarder la télévision. In the green armchair is my favorite place to watch television.

Vocabulary List for Chapter 7

La maison [may-z-on], the house/the home

Un appartement [ah-par-tuh-mon], an apartment

Le sous-sol [soo-soh-luh], the basement

Les escaliers [es-k-al-ee-ay], the stairs

Le toit [t-wah], the roof

La fenêtre [f-uh-n-eh-t-ruh], the window

La porte [p-oh-r-tuh], the door

La table [tah-b-luh], the table

Les rideaux [ree-doh], the curtains

Un tapis [tah-pee], a carpet / a rug

Le plafond [p-lah-f-on], the ceiling

Le mur [m-oo-ruh], the wall

L'arrière-cour [ah-ree-air-k-oo-r], the backyard

Le porche [p-oh-r-sh], the porch

La boîte aux lettres [b-wah-tuh][oh][l-eh-t-ruh], the mailbox

Le pont [p-oh-n], the deck

La cuisine [k-wee-z-ee-n], the kitchen

Ma maison est très réconfortante après une longue journée. My house is very comforting/soothing after a long day.

Réconfortante [ray-kon-for-ton-tuh]

Longue [l-on-g]

Journée [j-oo-r-nay]

Mon mari a acheté la table et le tapis hier soir. My husband bought the table and the carpet yesterday night.

Acheter [ah-sh-eh-tay]

Hier [yee-air]

Soir [s-wah-ruh]

Je construis le pont avec mon fils. I am building the deck with my son.

Construis [k-on-s-t-r-wee]

Le réfrigérateur [ray-f-ree-j-air-ah-t-ur], the refrigerator

Le frigo [f-ree-go], the fridge (this term is more of a slang word)

Un four [f-oo-r], an oven

Une fourchette [f-oor-sh-eh-t], a fork

Un couteau [k-oo-t-oh], a knife

Une cuillere [k-wee-air], a spoon

Une chaise [sh-ez], a chair

La table à manger [t-ah-b-luh][ah][mon-j-ay], the dining table

Je vais à la cuisine pour manger. I am going to the kitchen to eat.

Vais [v-ay]

J'aime manger la soupe avec une cuillère. I like eating soup with a spoon.

Soupe [s-oo-puh]

Je vais faire une tarte dans le four. I am going to make a pie in the oven.

Faire [f-air]

La chambre [sh-om-b-ruh], the bedroom

Une armoire [ar-m-wah-ruh], a closet

Un lit [lee], a bed

Un oreiller [oh-ray-ay], a pillow

Un couvercle [koo-v-air-k-luh], a comforter

Le tapis tah-pee], the carpet

La commode [k-oh-moh-duh], the dresser

Je veux lire dans mon lit. I like reading in my bed.

Lire [lee-ruh]

J'aime mon nouveau couvercle avec les cercles bleus. I like my new comforter with blue circles.

Nouveau [noo-voh]

Cercles [s-air-k-luh]

Bleus [b-luh]

Je mis mes vêtements dans la commode. I put my clothes in the dresser.

Vêtements [v-et-mon]

La salle de bain [sah-luh][duh][ban], the bathroom

La toilette [t-wah-let], the toilet

Le lavabo [lah-vah-bo], the sink

La douche [doo-sh], the shower

La baignoire [bah-n-wah-ruh], the bathtub

Le miroir [mee-r-wah-r], the mirror

L'armoire de toilette [ar-m-wah-ruh][duh][t-wah-let], the bathroom cabinet

Je vais laver mes mains dans le lavabo. I'm going to wash my hands in the sink.

Laver [lah-vay]

Mains [m-ah-n]

Je me détends dans la baignoire. I relax / unwind in the bathtub.

Détend [day-ton]

Je dois aller à la toilette. In English, it means *I have to go to the toilet.*

Je Dois [j-uh][d-wah]

La salle de séjour [sah-luh][duh][say-j-oo-ruh], the living room

Le sofa, the couch

Le fauteuil [f-oh-toy], the armchair

La télévision [tay-lay-vee-z-yon], the television

La table basse [bah-suh], coffee table

Les jeux [j-uh] de société, board games

La console [k-on-soh-luh] de jeu, the game system

L'ordinateur [or-dee-nah-t-ur], the computer

Le bureau [b-you-row], the desk

Je fais mon travail de l'école au bureau. I do my school work at the desk.

Fais [fay]

Je joue les jeux de société avec mon père et mon frère chaque lundi soir. I play board games with my father and my brother every monday night.

Chaque [sh-ah-k]

Dans le fauteuil vert, c'est mon place préférée pour regarder la télévision. In the green armchair is my favorite place to watch television.

Regarder [ruh-g-ar-day]

Chapter 8: Animals

In this chapter, we will look at everything related to animals! We will break the terms and phrases down by types of animals, and the chapter will also include sample sentences for you to practice with.

House Animals/Pets

Animal de compagnie, house pet

Un chien, a dog

Un chat, a cat

Un poisson, a fish

Un lapin, a rabbit

Un oiseau, a bird

Une araignée, a spider

Un hamster, a hamster

Jacques a une araignée comme animal de compagnie. Jacques has a pet snake.

J'ai deux poissons, un s'appelle bulle et l'autre s'appelle eau. I have two fish, one is named bubble, and the other is named water.

Un lapin a sauté dans mon arrière-cour. A rabbit jumped in my backyard.

Farm Animals

Animaux de ferme, farm animals

Animal de ferme, farm animal

Cheval, horse

Vache, cow

Mouton, sheep

Poule, hen / chicken

Chèvre, goat

Coq, rooster

Poussin, chick

Cochon, pig

Canard, duck

Dinde, turkey

Mon cheval peut sauter très haut. My horse can jump very high.

Le coq cri dans le matin. The rooster screams in the morning.

La poule ponde les œufs délicieux. The chicken lays delicious eggs.

Zoo Animals

Tigre, tiger

Eléphant, elephant

Girafe, giraffe

Lion, Lion

Guépard, cheetah

Kangourou, kangaroo

Singe, monkey

Chameau, camel

Hippopotame, hippopotamus

Ours, bear

Hibou, owl

Pingouin, penguin

Faucon, falcon

Autruche, ostrich

Requin, shark

Baleine, whale

Dauphin, dolphin

Crocodile, crocodile

Tortue, turtle

Grenouille, frog

J'ai vu un tigre et un lion qui était amis. I saw a tiger and a lion that were friends.

Le faucon a volé au-dessus de ma tête. The falcon flew over my head.

Le crocodile cache dans l'eau boueuse. The crocodile hides in the sludgy water.

Other Animals

Souris, mouse

Cygne, swan

Renard, fox

Loup, wolf

Rat, rat

Chauve-souris, bat

Écureuil, squirrel

Serpent, snake

Lézard, lizard

Abeille, bee

Mouche, fly

Moustique, mosquito

Papillon, butterfly

Fourmi, ant

Ver, worm

Escargot, snail

Les fourmis travaillent ensembles. The ants work together.

L'écureuil mange les noix qu'il trouve dans la rue. The squirrel eats the nuts that it finds in the road.

Un rat et un souris semble très similaire. A rat and a mouse look very similar.

More Sentence Examples

J'aime beaucoup visiter les animaux de ferme. I love visiting the farm animals.

Mon frère veut un serpent comme animaux de compagnie mais mes parents disent non. My brother wants a pet snake, but my parents said no.

Sophie ne veut pas regarder les singes au zoo. Sophie doesn't like looking at the monkeys in the zoo.

Les verres sortent de la terre quand il pleut, car le terre devient très mouillée. The worms come out of the ground when it rains because the ground becomes very wet.

Vocabulary List for Chapter 8

Animal de compagnie [ah-nee-mah-luh][duh][k-om-pah-nee], house pet

Chien [sh-yen], dog

Chat [sh-ah], cat

Hamster, hamster [ahm -st-air]

Serpent [s-air-pon-t], snake

Cheval [sh-eh-va-l], horse

Souris [s-oo-ree], mouse

Un poisson [p-wah-s-oh-nuh], a fish

Un oiseau [wah-z-oh], a bird

Un lapin [lah-pah-nuh], a rabbit

Une araignée [ah-rah-n-yay], a spider

Jacques a une araignée comme animal de compagnie. Jacques has a pet snake.

Comme [k-um]

J'ai deux poissons, un s'appelle bulle et l'autre s'appelle eau. I have two fish, one is named bubble, and the other is named water.

S'appelle [s-ah-p-eh-luh]

Bulle [boo-luh]

Eau [oh]

Un lapin a sauté dans mon arrière-cour. A rabbit jumped in my backyard.

Sauté [s-oh-tay]

Animaux de ferme [ah-nee-m-oh][duh][f-eh-r-m-uh], farm animals

Animal de ferme [ah-nee-mah-luh][duh][f-eh-r-m-uh], farm animal

Cheval [sh-eh-vah-luh], horse

Chèvre [sh-eh-v-ruh], goat

Cochon [k-oh-sh-on], pig

Vache [v-ah-sh], cow

Mouton [m-oo-toh-n], sheep

Poule [p-oo-luh], hen / chicken

Coq [k-oh-k], rooster

Poussin [poo-s-an], chick

Canard [k-ah-n-ar-d], duck

Dinde [d-an-d], turkey

Mon cheval peut sauter très haut. My horse can jump very high.

Sauter [s-oh-tay]

Haut [oh-t]

Le coq cri dans le matin. The rooster screams in the morning.

Cri [k-ree]

Matin [m-ah-t-ah-n]

La poule ponde les œufs délicieux. The chicken lays delicious eggs.

Ponde [p-on-duh]

Tigre [tee-g-ruh], tiger

Eléphant [ay-lay-f-on], elephant

Girafe [gee-rah-f], giraffe

Lion [lee-on], Lion

Guépard [gay-p-ar], cheetah

Kangourou [k-on-goo-roo], kangaroo

Singe [s-an-j], monkey

Chameau [sh-ah-mo], Camel

Hippopotame [ee-poh-poh-t-ah-muh], hippopotamus

Ours [oo-r-s], bear

Hibou [ee-boo], owl

Pingouin [pan-goo-wan], penguin

Faucon [f-oh-k-on], falcon

Autruche [oh-tree-sh], ostrich

Requin [ruh-k-in], shark

Baleine [bah-leh-n], whale

Dauphin [doh-f-en], dolphin

Crocodile [k-roh-k-oh-dee-luh], crocodile

Tortue [tor-too], turtle

Grenouille [g-ren-wee], frog

J'ai vu un tigre et un lion qui était amis. I saw a tiger and a lion who were friends.

Amis [ah-mee]

Le faucon a volé au-dessus de ma tête. The falcon flew over my head.

Volé [v-oh-lay]

Tête [t-eh-tuh]

Le crocodile cache dans l'eau boueuse. The crocodile hides in the muddy water.

Cache [k-ah-sh]

Boueux [boo-uh]

Souris [soo-ree], mouse

Cygne [see-nuh], swan

Renard [ruh-nar], fox

Loup [loo], wolf

Rat [rah], rat

Chauve-souris [sh-oh-v][soo-ree], bat

Écureuil [ay-koo-roy], squirrel

Serpent [sair-pon], Snake

Lézard [lay-z-ar], lizard

Abeille [ah-bay], bee

Mouche [moo-sh], fly

Moustique [moo-s-tee-k], mosquito

Papillon [pah-pee-on], butterfly

Fourmi [foo-r-mee], ant

Ver [v-air], worm

Escargot [es-k-ar-goh], snail

Les fourmis travaillent ensembles. Ants work together.
Ensembles [on-som-b-l-uh]

L'écureuil mange les noix qu'il trouve dans la rue. The squirrel eats the nuts it finds on the street.
Noix [n-wah]
Trouve [t-roo-v]

Un rat et un souris semble très similaire. A rat and a mouse look very similar.
Semble [s-om-b-luh]

J'aime beaucoup visiter les animaux de ferme. I really like visiting farm animals.
Visiter [vee-see-tay]

Mon frère veut un serpent comme animaux de compagnie mais mes parents disent non. My brother wants a snake as a pet, but my parents say no.

Disent [dee-z]

Les verres sortent de la terre quand il pleut, car le terre devient très mouillée. Glasses come out of the ground when it rains, because the soil gets very wet.

Sortent [s-or-t]

Terre [t-air]

Quand [k-on-d]

Devient [d-uh-vee-yen]

Mouille [moo-yay]

Chapter 9: How to Ask for Information and Help With the Language

As much as you practice and learn, there will come a time when you need to ask someone for clarification or for some help with the language. This section will deal with those types of questions, so if there's a need, you can ask for help. There is no need to be ashamed if this happens to you; asking questions like this will help you learn!

The first one we will look at is *Je ne comprends pas*, translated to "I don't understand" in English Let's hope that you don't need to use this one too much, but if you don't understand someone's French when they are speaking too fast, or if you don't understand the concept in general, you can say this to them.

If you forget a word, or you need to ask someone how to say something specific in French, you can ask them, *Comment dit-on … en francais?* And then insert the thing that you are asking them in place of the three dots. What this means is, "How do we say… In French." For example, you can ask them, *"Comment dit-on doughnut en francais?* [coh-mon][dee-t][ohn]doughnut[ohn][f-ron-say], which means "How do you say 'doughnut' in French?" It is okay that the word you are asking about is in

English; the person will be appreciative that you are trying to ask them in French, save for the word you are unsure about.

If someone asks you a question, and you don't know the answer, you can say *Je ne sais pas*, which means "I don't know." This will be helpful if someone asks you for directions in a foreign place or if someone asks you if you know someone. This is quite a versatile phrase, just like in the English language.

If you want to ask someone a question about something (pretty much anything), you can usually begin by saying *Quel est...?* This simply translates to "What is...," depending on the context. You will use this if you want to ask a person what something is, which you could ask by saying *Qu'est-ce que c'est?* This literally means, "What is that?" For example, this could be used when pointing to something in a museum or in a coffee shop.

You can use this phrase similarly to the one we learned earlier: *Comment dit-on ... en francais?* But this one could instead be used to ask for the English translation of a certain word. For example, you could use the expression *Qu'est-ce que (insert the word in French that you aren't sure of the meaning) en anglais?* This could be something like *Qu'est-ce que c'est l'hiver?* You can use this if you don't know the meaning of the word they just said. Then, they will respond to your question by saying something like *L'hiver* c'est *winter en anglais*.

If you are okay with the language and most of the words that they are saying, but you just didn't hear them because of the low volume or their accent, you can use the expression *S'il vous plaît dites-le encore*, which is how you say, "Please say it again." This is a respectful and polite way of asking someone to repeat themselves. If you want to directly ask them to repeat themselves instead of just saying "sorry?" or "I didn't understand," you can ask them this way instead. Or you can ask, *Pouvez-vous répéter ça, s'il vous plaît?* As we learned earlier, using *vous* is a more polite way to address someone, and using *tu* is a less formal way that you would use with friends.

As we briefly touched on in that last paragraph, sometimes, you want to ask someone what they have just said by saying, "sorry?" like we would in English. Here, we will learn how to do so.

This is done by saying *Pardon?* This can be used in a variety of ways, either to ask someone politely to repeat themselves or as a statement if you wish to apologize to someone. You can use this when you are squeezing by someone at the movie theatre when you go to the bathroom during the film and if you want someone to repeat what they said because you didn't hear them. You can also use it if you want to apologize to someone.

Another but more specific way to ask someone to repeat themselves is by saying *plus lentement*, which translates to "slower." You can use this phrase to ask someone to repeat themselves but to speak slower if you are having trouble understanding them. This could be because of a different accent than you are used to or because they are speaking too fast for you to understand. *Plus lentement* actually directly translates to "more slowly." If you want to make it even more polite, like if you have just met the person or they are working at a restaurant you are visiting, for example, you can say *s'il vous plait* at the end of this phrase and form it as a question. *Plus lentement, s'il vous plait.*

Another polite way to ask someone to repeat themselves is to say *encore Une fois*, which means "one more time." This can be used similarly to the above phrase, but this one is used to ask someone to repeat themselves in a different way. This way doesn't mean that you want them to speak slower; it's more useful when you just simply did not hear someone. If you want them to repeat themselves but in a slower voice, be sure to use the previous phrase instead. This one can be used if you are in a loud place and cannot hear someone or if they mumbled their words. Someone may say this phrase to you if they are having some trouble understanding your accent, but don't worry, just press on and repeat yourself.

If you want to ask someone for help for anything, you can say *Est-ce que vous pouvez m'aider?* which means "Can you help me?" This one is a good one to know because it can be used in virtually any situation where you may need help, whether it is with directions, with a question about the language, like we learned above, or something more serious, like needing help in an emergency. Keep this one closer to the front of your mind just in case you need help with anything.

If you want to ask someone to help you with information in a polite but more specific way than the above example, you can say the following:

Excusez-moi Monsieur/Madame? Est-ce que vous pouvez m'aider?

Then, they will likely say something like *Oui, bien-sur!* which means "yes, certainly!" or "Yes, of course!" Then, you will say one of the following options:

Est-ce que vous pouvez me dire... Could you tell me...

Est-ce que vous pouvez m'expliquer... Could you explain to me...

Pouvez-vous me montrer... Kindly show me...

Then, you can follow any of these with what you need them to tell, show, or explain to you. Below, I have written out some example sentences for you to see how this conversation would go in reality.

Est-ce que vous pouvez me dire pourquoi c'est si froid dans ma chambre? Could you tell me why it's so cold in my room?

Est-ce que vous pouvez me montrer comment changer la température dans ma chambre? Could you show me how to change the temperature in my room?

Est-ce que vous pouvez m'expliquer ce système de transport public? Could you explain to me this public transit system?

Vocabulary List for Chapter 9

Je ne comprends pas [j-uh][nuh][k-om-p-ron-d][pah]

Comment dit-on ... en francais?

Comment dit-on doughnut en français? [coh-mon][dee-t][ohn]doughnut[oh-n][f-ron-say]

Je ne sais pas [j-uh][nuh][say][pah]

Qu'est-ce que c'est? [k-ess][kuh]say]

Qu'est-ce que c'est (insert word in French that you aren't sure of the meaning of) en anglais?

"L'hiver c'est winter en anglais."

Répétez, s'il vous plaît

Pardon? [pa-r-doh-n] (rolled r)

Plus lentement [p-loo][lon-tuh-mon-t]

Plus lentement, s'il vous plaît.

Encore Une fois [on-k-or][oo-n][f-wah]

Est-ce que vous pouvez me dire [dee-ruh]... Could you tell me...

Est-ce que vous pouvez me montrer [mon-t-ray]... Could you show me...

Est-ce que vous pouvez m'expliquer [m-ex-p-lee-kay]... Could you explain to me...

Est-ce que vous pouvez me dire pourquoi c'est si froid dans ma chambre? Can you tell me why it's so cold in my room?

Froid [f-r-wah]

Est-ce que vous pouvez me montrer comment changer la température dans ma chambre? Can you show me how to change the temperature in my room?

Comment [k-om-on]

Changer [sh-on-j-ay]

Est-ce que vous pouvez m'expliquer ce système de transport public? Can you explain to me this public transit system?

Publique [poo-b-lee-k]

Chapter 10: To Go Shopping

Shopping is a big attraction when visiting any new city, and if you are visiting any French-speaking city, you will surely need to know how to ask the staff for anything you may need, how to read the tags, and what the signs around the store may mean. This chapter will teach you all of this and more.

Before you go shopping, these terms will help you determine where you will shop. Will you shop in a department store, in a shopping mall, or at a market? Read below for the words to say regarding the types of stores and those that concern the general act of shopping.

Un Grand Magasin, a department store

Un Centre commerciale, a shopping mall

Un marché, a market

Faire du shopping, to shop / to go shopping

Faire du lèche-vitrine, to window shop / to go window shopping

Une Solde, a sale

Portefeuille, wallet

Bon Shopping! Happy shopping / Enjoy shopping!

Acheter, to buy

Vendre, to sell

Once you are shopping, you may hear some of these things from either the people you are shopping with or the store employees, and you may also want to ask them some of the following questions.

Est-ce que c'est en solde? Is this on sale?

Bon marché, good deal / cheap

Meilleur marché que..., a better deal than...

Une bonne affaire, a good deal

C'est combien? How much does this cost?

Ou sont les cabines? Where are the change rooms?

Puis-je emprunter un miroir? Can I borrow a mirror?

Je vais essayer... I am going to try on...

C'est trop serre. It's too tight.

J'aime celui-ci le plus. I like this one the best.

Ce me plait beaucoup. I like this a lot.

Je vais le prendre I am going to get this

J'ai envie d'acheter celui-ci. I want to buy this one.

Vous fermez à quelle heure? What time do you close?

Vous êtes ouvert demain? Are you open tomorrow?

A store employee may come up and ask you if you need any help by saying *Avez-vous besoin de quelque chose?* This means, "Do you need something?" They may also ask you something like *Avez-vous besoin d'aide pour trouver quelque chose?* which means, "Do you need any help finding something?" You can respond in a number of ways, one of which is by saying *Non, merci, je regarde simplement*. What this means is, "No, thank you. I'm just looking" or "I'm just browsing." If you do want help, you can say *Oui, merci. Je cherche...* This means "Yes, thank you. I am looking for..." Then you will insert whatever you are looking for. Examples of this are below.

Oui merci, je cherche une robe noire. Yes, thank you. I am looking for a black dress.

Oui merci, je cherche des/les souliers. Yes, thank you. I am looking for (the) shoes.

Oui merci, je cherche les lunettes de soleil. Yes, thank you, I am looking for the sunglasses.

Oui merci, je cherche un cadeau pour ma petite amie. Yes, thank you. I am looking for a gift for my girlfriend.

Notice in the above sentence examples how there is either the word *les* or *des* that precedes the thing you are looking for. There is a slight difference between these, which I will explain now. *Les* is used in a more specific sense, as in "the shoes," which implies that you are looking for the shoe section specifically. If you said *des souliers,* however, this would mean "some shoes," which is less specific and implies that you are loosely looking around for some shoes. Note this distinction as you practice creating some sentences of your own.

If you are looking for something specific, you can also ask the employee to help you find this. For example, if you are looking at a shirt that you like but you want to know if they have any other sizes or colors, you can ask them this by saying, *Est-ce que vous l'avez...* This means, "Do you have it in..." You will insert the word in place of the three dots. Some examples of this are below.

Est-ce que vous l'avez en rouge?

Est-ce que vous l'avez en taille petit?

Est-ce que vous l'avez en taille 29?

Notice how the word *taille* is used here; this means "size." If you are looking for a certain size, you will say "size small."

After you pay, or when you are going up to pay for your items, the following phrases will come in handy for you.

Je vais à la caisse. I am going to pay

S'il vous plaît donnez-moi un sac. Please give me a bag.

Est-ce que vous avez un sac en plastique? Do you have a plastic bag?

Est-ce que vous prenez les cartes de crédit? Do you take credit cards?

La carte de débit est-elle acceptable? Can I pay by debit card?

Sometimes, you will need to exchange or return something. The sentences below will show you how to do this.

Je voudrais échanger celui-ci s'il vous plaît. I would like to exchange this, please

This next sentence is similar but asking for a refund instead:

Je voudrais retourner celui-ci s'il vous plaît. I want to return this one, please.

Vocabulary List for Chapter 10

Un Grand Magasin [g-ron][mah-gah-z-ah-n], a department store

Un Centre commerciale [s-on-t-ruh][k-om-air-see-ah-luh], a shopping mall

Un marché [m-ah-r-sh-ay], a market

Faire du shopping [f-air][d-oo], to shop / to go shopping

Faire du lèche-vitrine [l-eh-sh][vee-t-ree-nuh], to window shop / to go window shopping

Une Solde [soh-l-duh], a sale

Portefeuille [poh-r-tuh-f-oy], wallet

Bon [b-oh-nuh] Shopping! Happy shopping / enjoy shopping!

Acheter [ah-sh-tay], to buy

Vendre [v-on-d-ruh], to sell

Est-ce disponible en vente? Is this on sale?

Est-ce [ess-suh]

Meilleur marché que..., A better deal than...

Meilleur [may-uh-ruh]

Une bonne affaire, A good deal

Affaire [ah-fay-ruh]

C'est combien? How much does this cost?

132

Combien [k-om-bee-en]

Est-ce que je peux vous aider?

Peux [p-uh]

Non, merci, je regarde simplement.

Regarde [r-uh-g-ar-d-uh]

Vous cherchez quelque chose?

Cherchez [sh-air-sh-ay]

Oui, merci. Je cherche [wee][m-air-see][juh][sh-air-sh]

Oui merci, je cherche une robe noire. Yes, thank you. I am looking for a black dress.

Noir [n-wah-ruh]

Oui merci, je cherche des/les souliers. Yes, thank you, I am looking for (the) shoes

Souliers [soo-lee-ay]

Oui merci, je cherche les lunettes de soleil. Yes, thank you, I am looking for the sunglasses.

Lunettes [loo-n-eh-t]

Oui merci, je cherche un cadeau pour ma petite amie. Yes, thank you. I am looking for a gift for my girlfriend.

Cadeau [k-ah-d-oh]

Les [lay]

Des [day]

Est-ce que vous l'avez en rouge?

L'avez [l-av-ay]

Rouge [roo-j]

Est-ce que vous l'avez en taille petit?

Taille [t-eye]

Petit [p-uh-tee]

I am going to pay, Je vais à la caisse

Caisse [k-ah-suh]

S'il vous plaît donnez-moi un sac en papier. Please give me a paper bag.

Papier [pah-pee-ay]

Est-ce que vous prenez les cartes de crédit? Do you take credit cards?

Prenez [p-ruh-nay]

Est-ce que je peux payer par carte bancaire? Can I pay by debit card?

Bancaire [bon-kee-air]

Je voudrais échanger celui-ci s'il vous plaît. I want to exchange this please.

Échanger [ay-sh-on-j-ay]

Je voudrais retourner celui-ci. I want to return this one.

Celui-ci [sell-wee-see]

Chapter 11: Restaurant/Coffee

We will now look at the process of ordering food from a restaurant, as it is slightly different in French than in English. After reading through this section and practicing it a few times, you will be all set to begin visiting French restaurants and any other restaurant in French-speaking places! To begin, we will look at the names of the meals themselves that you may need to know when you are reading a menu. First, if you want to reserve a table at a restaurant, you can do so by calling on the phone in most cases. The conversation would look something like this:

Bonjour, Restaurant _____ C'est Pierre.

Bonjour, je voudrais réserver une table s'il vous plaît.

Pour combien de personnes?

Pour deux personnes

Pour quand?

Pour demain soir à dix-huit heures

A quel nom?

Giroux.

D'accord, a demain Monsieur Giroux!

Merci, beaucoup

The translation for this phone dialogue is below:

"Hello, _____ Restaurant, Pierre Speaking."

"Hello, I would like to reserve a table, please."

"For how many people?"

"For two people."

"For when?"

"For tomorrow night at 18:00."

"Under what name?"

"Giroux"

"Right. See you tomorrow, Mr. Giroux!"

"Thank you very much."

Then, when you arrive at the restaurant, in order to find your reservation, you will say:

Bonjour, est-ce que vous avez la réservation?

Bonjour, bien sûr! J'ai actuellement réservé une table hier pour deux personnes au nom de Giroux.

Bon, suivez-moi

The translation for this in-person dialogue is below:

"Hello, do you have a reservation?"

"Hello, yes. I reserved a table for two people under the name Giroux."

"Great, follow me."

Un restaurant, a restaurant

Le menu, **the** *menu*

Un menu, **a** *menu*

L'entrée / L'hors d'oeuvre, the appetizer

Le plat principal, the main course

Le dessert, dessert

À la carte, from the menu

Prix fixe, set menu

Le fromage, cheese plate

Le digestif, after-dinner drink

When you enter the restaurant, there will likely be a sign saying *Asseyez-vous memes*, which means "seat yourselves." If you don't see this, someone will likely lead you to your seat. If you are just checking out a restaurant to see if you'd like to eat there, you can ask for a menu when you enter by saying, *Bonjour, est-ce que je puex avoir Une carte, s'il vous plaît*, which means, "Hello, could I have a menu, please." Once you are seated, you may need to ask for extra things or some clarification regarding the menu. This section will walk you through all of these possible things.

This first section deals with the words you may need to know when ordering your food.

Je voudrais, I would like…

Plat Du jour, spécial / dish of the day

Le serveur, server / waiter

À point, medium rare

La serveuse, waitress

Végétalien, vegan

Végétarien, vegetarian

Compris/Inclus, included

Bleu, saignant: rare ("blue" or "bleeding")

Bien cuit, well done

À votre goût, to your liking

Frit(e), fried

Un morceau, a piece

Haché, ground (meat)

Fumé, smoked

Un méli-mélo, an assortment

Rôti: roasted

Piquant: spicy

Provençal, cooked with tomatoes, anchovies, and olives

À la vapeur, steamed

This section now will look at things you may need once you receive your food or while you are eating.

Le vin, wine

Le sel [luh][s-el], the salt

La Biere, beer

Le poivre [luh][p-wah-v-ruh], the pepper

Des serviettes [day][s-air-vee-et-s], napkins

De l'eau [duh][l-oh], some water

Du café [doo][kah-fay], some coffee

Du Thé [doo][tay], some tea

Le ketchup [luh]ketchup, the ketchup

Le sauce piquante [luh][soh-s][pee-k-ont], the hot sauce

Allergique à, allergic to

L'assiette, plate

Délicieux, delicious

Une tranche, a slice

You can ask for any of the above items by saying the word, followed by *s'il vous plaît* [seel][voo][p-l-ay], which means "please."

One thing to note is that the word *garçon* means "boy," and *Fille* means "girl." You may have heard this being used in the movies when a restaurant scene comes on. However, this is considered very rude in French. What you should say in order to get the attention of the waiter is *Excusez-moi monsieur* or *Excusez-moi madame*.

When you finish eating, they may come around and offer to take your plate. If this is the case, you can say *C'est terminé*, which means "It's finished" or "The plate is finished."

If you are ready for your bill, you can say, *L'addition, s'il vous plaît*. *L'addition* is *the bill* or *the check*. In a French restaurant, you will need to ask for the cheque when you are ready for it, as they will prefer not to make you feel like you are being asked to leave. So when you are about to leave, you can use these phrases to ask for it:

L'addition, the bill

Le pourboire, the tip

After they bring you anything or when you are leaving, and you want to thank them, you will say:

Merci [meh-r-see], Thank you

Merci beaucoup [meh-r-see][b-oh-k-oo], Thanks a lot, thank you so much

Merci bien [meh-r-see][bee-yen], Thank you very much

If you want to be more formal when you say thank you, you can say "thank you, sir" or "thank you, ma'am."

You can also combine any of the above ways of saying thank you with *sir* or *ma'am* to be extra polite, for example:

Merci Monsieur [meh-r-see][moh-see-uh-r], Thank you, Sir

Merci Madame [meh-r-see][mah-dah-m], Thank you, ma'am

Merci Beaucoup Madame [meh-r-see][b-oh-k-oo][mah-dah-m], Thank you so much, ma'am.

EXERCISE

Try an exercise now to practice this.

You just walked into a restaurant, and you see a sign saying, "Asseyez-vous memes." You then walked into the dining room and sat at a small, round table. When you see a waiter walk by, you catch her eye because you want to ask her for the menu. When she stops at your table, you say, _____. After you have looked at the menu, you decide that you want to order a coffee. When the waitress comes by you again, you say, _____.

Then, after drinking your coffee, you decide that you need some sugar (*du sucre* [soo-k-ruh]), so you say _____. Once you finish your coffee, you are ready for your bill. You call the waitress over by saying, _____. You then ask her for the bill by saying, _____. Then, you pay your bill, and you are ready to leave. As you are walking out the door, you say, _____.

(The answers to this quiz can be found in the vocabulary list at the end of this chapter).

Coffee Shop

Un café

Un café au lait

Un café allongé

Un café décaféiné

Un café noisette

Un café américain

Café filtré

Un café glacé

Du thé

Un thé glacé

Un thé vert

Un thé noir

Chocolat chaud

Du lait s'il vous plaît

Du Sucre s'il vous plaît

Now, in either a restaurant or a coffee shop, there are slightly different ways to go about ordering. First, you will say either:

Je voudrais, I would like or *Je prendrai, I will take*

If you are not ready to order yet and you need another minute, you will say:

Je n'ai pas encore choisi, I haven't chosen yet.

Or

Une minute encore s'il vous plaît

We will look at some examples below.

Je prendrai un bifteck bien cuit s'il vous plaît. I will take a steak well done, please

Je voudrais un chocolat chaud s'il vous plaît. I would like a hot chocolate, please

On prendrait deux cafés américaines. We will take two filter coffees.

Nous voudrions trois tasses de bière. We would like three glasses of beer.

Vocabulary List for Chapter 11

Bonjour [boh-n-j-oo-r], Restaurant _____ C'est [s-ay] Pierre.

Bonjour, je voudrais réserver une table [t-ah-b-luh] s'il vous plaît.

Pour combien [k-om-bee-yen] de personnes?

Pour deux personnes

Pour quand [k-on]?

Pour demain [duh-men] soir [s-wah-ruh] à dix-huit heure

A quel [k-el] nom [n-oh]?

Giroux [j-ee-roo].

D'accord, a demain Monsieur Giroux!

Merci, beaucoup

Bonjour, est-ce que vous avez la réservation?

Bonjour, bien sûr! J'ai actuellement réservé une table hier pour deux personnes au nom de Giroux.

Bon, suivez-moi [s-wee-vay-m-wah].

Un restaurant, a restaurant

Le menu [muh-noo], the menu

Le plat principal [p-lah][p-ran-see-pah-luh], the main course

Le dessert, dessert

À la carte [ah][lah][k-ar-tuh], from the menu

Prix fixe, set menu

Le fromage, cheese plate

Le digestif [dee-j-es-t-ee-fuh], after-dinner drink

Asseyez-vous mêmes, [ah-say-ay][voo][m-em]

Je voudrais, I would like…

Plat Du jour [p-lah][d-oo][j-oo-ruh], special / dish of the day

Le serveur/la serveuse [s-air-v-uh-z], waiter/waitress

Compris [k-om-p-ree]/Inclus, included

Bleu, saignant [say-n-ont], rare ("blue" or "bleeding")

À point [p-wah-n], medium rare

Bien cuit [b-ee-yen][k-wee], well done

À votre goût [voh-t-ruh][goo], to your liking

Frit [f-ree], fried

Fumé [foo-may], smoked

Haché [ah-shay], ground (meat)

Un méli-mélo [meh-lee-meh-loh], an assortment

Un morceau [moh-r-soh], a piece

Piquant [pee-k-on-tuh], spicy

Provençal [p-roh-von-s-al], Cooked with tomatoes, anchovies, and olives

Le sel [luh][s-el], the salt

Le poivre [luh][p-wah-v-ruh], the pepper

Des serviettes [day][s-air-vee-et-s], napkins

De l'eau [duh][l-oh], some water

Du café [doo][kah-fay], some coffee

Du The [doo][tay], some tea

Le ketchup [luh]ketchup, the ketchup

Le sauce piquante [luh][soh-s][pee-k-ont], the hot sauce

L'assiette [ass-ee-eh-tuh]: plate

Délicieux [day-lee-see-uh]: delicious

Une tranche [t-ron-sh]: a slice

Excusez-moi monsieur or *Excusez-moi madame*

C'est terminé [t-air-mee-nay]

L'addition, the bill

Le pourboire [poo-r-b-wah-ruh], the tip

Merci [meh-r-see]. Thank you.

Merci beaucoup [meh-r-see][b-oh-k-oo]. Thanks a lot / thank you so much.

Merci bien [meh-r-see][bee-yen]. Thank you very much.

If you want to be more formal when you say thank you, you can say "thank you, sir" or "thank you, ma'am." You can also combine any of the above ways of saying thank you with sir or ma'am to be extra polite, for example:

Merci Monsieur [meh-r-see][moh-see-uh-r]. Thank you, sir.

Merci Madame [meh-r-see][mah-dah-m]. Thank you, ma'am.

Merci Beaucoup Madame [meh-r-see][b-oh-k-oo][mah-dah-m]. Thank you so much, ma'am.

Answers to Chapter 11 Quiz

La carte,

Un cafe

Du sucre,

L'addition

Merci beaucoup madame

Coffee Shop

Un café

Un café allongé [ah-lon-j-ay]

Un café décaféiné

Un café au lait

Un café noisette [n-wah-s-eh-tuh]

Un café américain

Café filtré [feel-tray]

Un café glacé [g-lah-say]

Du thé [tay]

Un thé glacé

Un thé vert [v-air]

Un thé noir [n-wah-ruh]

Chocolat chaud [sh-oh-d]

Je prendrai [p-ron-d-ray]. I will take

C'est difficile de choisir. It's hard to choose.

Choisir [sh-wah-z-ee]

Je prendrai un bifteck bien cuit s'il vous plaît. I will take a steak, well done, please

Je voudrais un chocolat chaud. I would like hot chocolate.

On prendrait deux cafés américaines. We will take two filter coffees.

Nous voudrions trois tasses de bière. We would like three glasses of beer.

Tasses [tah-suh]

Chapter 12: Finding the Way/Directions

When traveling, finding your way is very important, and asking people you pass by on the street or people working in stores or hotels is very useful. Being able to ask people is not only important when you are in an English-speaking place but also when in a new place where they primarily speak another language that is not your own. With the knowledge gained in this chapter, you will be able to ask people for directions in French-speaking places in order to ensure you can get to where you are going with as little trouble as possible.

Addresses

We will now look at the way we say addresses in French. When we are talking about street addresses, there are a few differences between French and English. First, we will break it into pieces and look at each section contained in an address.

Streets

Rue [roo], street

Route [roo-t], road

Chemin [sh-uh-m-an], trail, path

Allee [ah-lay], driveway

Ruelle [roo-el], alley

Terrain de stationnement [tuh-r-an](rolled r)[duh][st-ah-si-on-mon-t], parking lot

Numbers

We will now look at the numbers from 1 to 10 in French. While there are differences in the way we say larger numbers, for your purposes, as long as you can say the numbers themselves, you will be fine. I will show you an example of what I mean below.

325 Example St.

Instead of having to say "three hundred and twenty five example street," as long as you can say "three two five example street," you will be able to adequately get your point across to the person you are asking, such as a taxi driver. As you now know, numbers from 1 to 20 and multiples of 10 from 20 to 100 (from learning about numbers in chapter 4), you will be able to say many many address numbers. If you aren't sure, however, you can simply state the numbers that you see that you do remember, and the person you are talking to will likely be able to understand what you are trying to say. As a refresher, the numbers from 1 to 10 are below for your reference.

1, 2, 3, 4, 5, 6, 7, 8, 9, 10

Un, deux, trois, quatre, cinq, six, sept, huit, neuf, dix

One, two, three, four, five, six, seven, eight, nine, ten

As an example, we will use the following address and look at it in more detail:

9 Rue Ste. Catherine

In French, when there is the word Saint, or St. in an address, like the street name *St. Catherine Street or St. Andrew street,* it is written as "Ste." instead of "St." like in English. This is because, in French, the word is *Sainte.* So when talking about any word or street with the word Saint in it, it will be written in this way:

Ste. Catherine, Sainte Catherine

Ste. Andrew, Sainte Andrew

Address Examples

When we write addresses, we write them in this order: number + street type (road, crescent, etc.) + street name. It is a bit of a different order than in English as the word street is moved to the front of the street name instead of after it.

9 St. Catherine Street is what we would say in English. In French, this would be written as *9 Rue Ste. Catherine* and said as *neuf, rue sainte catherine, à Paris, en France.*

13 Chemin Georges, un trois chemin georges, treize chemin georges. 13 Georges Street

100 chemin arbres, québec, québec, Canada. Cent chemin arbres, à québec, québec au Canada. 100 Arbres Trail, Quebec, Quebec, Canada.

À Washington vs. Au Washington

When we are talking about being or having been someplace, there are different ways to say this, depending on what type of place you're talking about. For example, in the United States, there are two different places called Washington. One is a state, and the other is a city. When speaking in English, we can tell which is being refered to because if they are talking about the state, they will say Washington State. In French, we don't do this, but there is another way that we can actually tell which of these somebody is talking about based on the word that precedes it. If we are talking about a city or town, we would say **À Washington**, which would indicate to the person we are speaking to that we are talking about the city. If we are talking about the state, we would say **Au Washington.**

One more thing to note is that if the province, state, or country we are talking about begins with a vowel, then using *au* would be quite a mouthful. In this case, we would say **en.** For example, "Je suis allé **en France**," which means, "I went to France." If you were talking about going to Paris, which is a city, you would say "Je suis allé **à Paris**."

Asking for Directions

This section will focus on the phrases you will need when you are traveling. These are related to transportation and directions so that you can get around with ease.

If you need to ask someone where something is, you can ask them in the following way:

Excusez-moi, est-ce que vous savez où est ____? This means Excuse me, do you know where is _____? You will then insert something like *La Tour Eiffel* (The Eiffel Tower.)

Like you learned earlier in this book, you could also say *Est ce que vous pouvez m'aider a trouver _____?* This means, "Could you help me find ____?"

Alternatively, you could also say *Est ce que vous savez ou est ce que c'est _____?* This means, "Do you know where _____ is?"

After asking this, you will likely hear one of the following responses:

Gauche, right

Droite, left

C'est..., It is / It's...

C'est à droite, It's to the right

C'est à gauche, It's to the left

C'est à côté de [s-eh][ah][k-oh-tay][duh], It's beside (something)

C'est près de [s-eh][pr-eh][duh], It's close to (something)

C'est près d'ici [s-eh][pr-eh][d-ee-see]], It's close to here

C'est loin d'ici [s-eh][l-w-ah-n][d-ee-see], It's far from here

C'est loin de [s-eh][l-w-ah-n][duh], It's far from (something)

Vocabulary List for Chapter 12

Excusez-moi, où [oo] est [ay] ____?

Est ce que vous pouvez [poo-vay] m'aider [ay-day] a trouver [t-roo-vay] _____?

Est ce que vous savez [sah-vay] ou est ce que c'est _____?

La Tour Eiffel [lah][too-r][ee-fell]

Gauche [g-oh-sh], right

Droite [dr-wah-tuh] (rolled r), left

C'est [s-eh], It is / It's

C'est à gauche. It's to the left.

C'est à droite. It's to the right.

C'est à côté de [s-eh][ah][k-oh-tay][duh]. It's beside (something).

C'est près de [s-eh][pr-eh][duh]. It's close to (something).

C'est près d'ici [s-eh][pr-eh][d-ee-see]]. It's close to here.

C'est loin de [s-eh][l-w-ah-n][duh]. It's far from (something).

C'est loin d'ici [s-eh][l-w-ah-n][d-ee-see]. It's far from here.

Rue [roo], street

Route [roo-t], road

Chemin [sh-uh-m-an], trail / path

Allee [ah-lay], driveway

Ruelle [roo-el], alley

Terrain de stationnement [tuh-r-an](rolled r)[duh][st-ah-si-on-mon-t], parking lot

1 [uhhn],

2 [duuh],

3 [t-r-wah] (rolled r),

4 [cat-ruh](rolled r),

5 [sank],

6 [see-s],

7 [set],

8 [wee-t],

9 [nuuf],

10 [dee-s]

9 Rue Ste. Catherine, 9 St. Catherine Street

Sainte

neuf, rue sainte catherine, a Paris en France

13 chemin georges, un trois chemin georges. 13 Georges Street

100 chemin arbres, québec, québec, Canada. Cent chemin arbres, à québec, québec au Canada. 100 Arbres Trail, Quebec, Quebec, Canada.

A Washington, to Washington (city)

Au Washington, to Washington State

Chapter 13: Modes of Transportation

In this chapter, we will look at various means of transportation and how you can refer to them in French, as well as some example sentences for you to practice. After you have read through this chapter, challenge yourself to make up some sentences of your own for practice.

We will begin by learning some terms related to transportation so that you know how to put these words into a sentence.

Prendre..., to take...

Assurer le service, to ensure service

Venir, to come

Aller, to go

Arriver, to arrive

En Avance, early

A l'heure, on time

En retard, late

First is the car. You will likely use this word quite often in conversations, as cars play such a big role in our lives, both when traveling and when at home. There are actually two different ways that you can talk about a car. The first and more common is *Une Auto,* and the second is *Une Voiture.* Both of these mean "a car," but the second is regarded as the correct form. If you are speaking to people to whom you want to show respect or those you don't know quite well, using the second option is best. When speaking to friends, feel free to use *l'auto* when saying "the car." This word can be used for a vehicle in general but is reserved for more casual conversations.

Monospace, minivan

Convertible, convertible

Un camion, a truck

Avion, airplane

Un hélicoptère, a helicopter

Le train, the train

L'autobus, the bus

Le Metro, The Subway / the Metro

Un taxi, a taxi

Un ferry, a ferry

Une Navette, a shuttle

À pied, on foot

Un bateau, a boat

Un canot, a canoe

Une Planche à roulette, a skateboard

Scooter, scooter

Une bicyclette, a bicycle

If you are talking about taking one of these modes of transportation above, you would say *par* before it in a sentence, which means "by way of." For example, *par avion, par autobus,* or *par voiture.* These mean "by way of airplane," "by way of bus," and "by way of car," respectively.

Example Sentences

We will now learn how to use these in a sentence so that you can begin using these terms right away!

Ma petite amie est arrivée par planche À roulette hier, mais elle a été deux heures en retard! My girlfriend arrived by way of skateboard yesterday, but she was two hours late!

Un hélicoptère peut être un mode de transport très amusant! A helicopter could be a very fun mode of transport!

J'ai un bateau à moteur et un canot. Le bateau à moteur est beaucoup plus vite que le canot. I have a motor boat and a canoe. The motor boat is much faster than the canoe.

Le train est arrivé quinze minutes en avance et j'ai été heureux parce que j'ai voulu m'asseoir pendant que j'attendais le train quitté vers ma maison. The train arrived fifteen minutes early, and I was happy because I wanted to sit down while I waited for it to leave for my house.

Vocabulary List for Chapter 13

Prendre [p-ron-d-ruh] ..., to take...

Assurer la service, to ensure service

Venir [vuh-neer], to come

Aller [ah-lay], to go

En Avance [ah-von-suh], early

A l'heure, on time

En retard [ruh-tar-duh], late

Monospace [moh-no-s-pah-suh], minivan

Convertible, convertible

Un camion [k-ah-mee-on], a truck

Avion, airplane

Un hélicoptère, a helicopter

Le train, the train

L'autobus, the bus

Le Metro, the subway / the Metro

Un taxi, a taxi

Un ferry, a ferry

Une Navette, a shuttle

À pied [pee-ay], on foot

Un bateau [bah-toh], a boat

Un canot [k-ah-no], a canoe

Une Planche à roulette, a skateboard

Scooter, scooter

Un bicyclette, a bicycle

par avion

par autobus

par voiture

Ma petite amie est arrivée par planche À roulette hier, mais elle a été deux heures en retard! My girlfriend arrived by way of skateboard yesterday, but she was two hours late!
Hier [yee-air]

Un hélicoptère peut être un mode de transport très amusant! A helicopter could be a very fun mode of transport!
Amusant [ah-moo-son-tuh]

J'ai un bateau à moteur et un canot. Le bateau à moteur est beaucoup plus vite que le canot. I have a motor boat and a canoe. The motor boat is much faster than the canoe.
Vite [vee-tuh]

Le train est arrivé quinze minutes en avance et j'ai été heureux parce que j'ai voulu m'asseoir pendant que j'attendais le train quitté vers ma maison. The train arrived fifteen minutes early, and I was happy because I wanted to sit down while I waited for it to leave for my house.

Heureux [her-uh]

Vers [v-air]

Chapter 14: Travel, Transportation, and How to Book/Buy a Ticket

Buying a Ticket

This section will tell you how to buy a ticket and other phrases that will come in handy when you need to travel and find your way around transportation in general. We will look at a variety of scenarios, and you will be well on your way to traveling around with ease.

The first thing we will look at is the metro, the train, or a bus. These types of transportation will require you to buy a ticket before you get on, so you will need to know how to buy a ticket or how to ask for help if you aren't sure how. We will first look at some words that you will come across in the stations and on signs leading to these stations.

Un Billet [bee-yay], a ticket

Les Billets, tickets

You will likely see a sign that says, *Guichet de la Billetterie,* which means "Ticketing Counter." This is where you will go with your ticket questions or buy a ticket. When you get to the counter, you will say *Bonjour, je veux acheter un billet,* which means, "Hello, I would like to buy a ticket." *Un billet* (a ticket) *s'il vous plaît* (please), which means, "One ticket, please" will also work. If you want to be more specific, you can specify where exactly you are going so that you can get a ticket to the right place. To do this, you will insert the name of the place you are going or the station you want to get to right after the word "ticket," such as *Un billet <u>à Paris</u> s'il vous plaît.*

When it comes to buying tickets, if you are doing so at a counter or even online, the following terms will help you to ensure you clearly understand what you are buying so that you end up in the right place!

Un billet aller-retour, a return ticket

Un billet aller-simple, a one-way ticket

Un siège, a seat

Je voudrais réserver un billet. I would like to reserve a ticket.

Je dois acheter un billet de retour pour la Grèce. I need to buy a return ticket to Greece.

S'il vous plaît réservez-moi le vol de 21 heures. Please book me the 9 PM flight.

Payer par carte bancaire, pay by debit

Combien coûte le billet? In English, this means, *How much does the ticket cost?*

Donnez-vous un rabais pour une personne âgée? Qu'en est-il d'un étudiant? Do you give a discount for a senior? What about a student?

Avez-vous de rabais pour une personne plus âgée? Do you have a discount for a senior person?

Je dois arriver à quelle heure? What time should I arrive?

When you are ready to go to the station for your train, bus, or flight, you can say to your taxi driver one of the following:

Je veux aller à l'aéroport. I want to go to the airport

Est-ce que vous pouvais me conduire à la station de train/ à la gare? Can you drive me to the train station?

Station de train/gare, train station

Station d'autobus, bus station

Aéroport, airport

Then, once you get to the station, you can ask for directions by saying:

Est-ce que vous pouvais m'aider à trouver ma porte? What this means is, "Can you help me find my gate?"

J'ai un vol pour attraper, I have a flight to catch.

Checking In

When checking into a flight, you would call this *enregistrer*.

If you want to ask someone where you can go to check into your flight, you can ask for *la reception*. If you want to tell someone that you are looking for the check-in desk, you can say, *je veux me presenter a la reception.* Once you get there, you will want to tell them that you have a reservation. To say this, you will say *J'ai une reservation.*

Upon check-in, you will be able to ask any questions, and you will be able to check your bags there. When they ask you which bags are for check-in, you will say:

J'ai une valise et trois sacs à main. I have one suitcase and three carry-on bags.

You can substitute this with any other number, as you learned previously in this book.

When you get to where you are going, you would say that you or someone else has:

Arriver, to arrive

More Travel Words and Phrases

Voyager, to travel

Un Passeport, a passport

Une Valise, a suitcase

Les bagages, baggage

Un plan, a map

Sortie, exit

Entrée, entrance

Un Guide Touristique, a tour guide

Vocabulary List for Chapter 14

Un Billet [bee-yay], a ticket

Les Billets, Tickets

Guichet [gee-sh-ay] de la Billetterie, ticketing counter

Acheter[ah-sh-uh-tay] un billet, to buy a ticket

Un billet, s'il vous plaît [uhn][bee-yay][seel][v-oo][p-l-eh]

If you want to get more specific, you can specify where exactly you are going so that you can be sure you will get a ticket to the right place.

Un billet à <u>Paris</u> s'il vous plaît [uhn][bee-yay][ah][pah-ree][seel][v-oo][p-l-eh].

Un billet aller-retour [ah-lay-ruh-too-r], a return ticket

Un billet aller-simple [ah-lay-s-ah-m-p-luh], a one-way ticket

Un siège [see-y-eh-j], a seat

Je veux aller à la porte. I want to go to the gate

Je veux aller à l'aéroport. I want to go to the airport

Je veux réserver un billet. I would like to reserve a ticket.

Je dois acheter un billet de retour pour la Grèce. I need to buy a return ticket to Greece.

S'il vous plaît réservez-moi le vol de 21 heures. Please book me the 9 PM flight.

A quelle heure est ce que je dois [d-wah] arriver? What time should I arrive?

J'ai un valise et trois sacs à main. I have one suitcase and three carry-on bags.

Valise [vah-lee-suh]

Combien coûte le billet? How much should I pay for the ticket?

Combien [k-om-bee-yen]

Coûte [k-oo-tuh]

Donnez-vous un rabais pour une personne âgée? Qu'en est-il d'un étudiant? Do you give a discount for a senior? What about a student?

Rabais [rah-bay]

Etudiant [ay-tto-dee-y-on-t]

Avez-vous de rabais pour une personne plus âgée? Do you have a discount for a senior person?

Plus âgée, [p-loo][ah-j-ay]

Acheter un billet, to buy a ticket

J'ai un vol pour attraper

Vol [v-oh-l]

Payer par carte bancaire, pay by debit

Bancaire [b-on-k-ee-air]

Enregistrer [on-ray-gee-s-t-ray]

Voyager [v-oy-ah-j-ay], to travel

Un Passeport, a passport

Une Valise [v-ah-lee-z], a suitcase

Les bagages, baggage

Un plan, a map

Sortie, exit

Entrée [on-t-ray], entrance

Un Guide Touristique [g-ee-d][too-ree-s-t-ee-k], a tour guide

Chapter 15: Hotels and Accomodations

When you go to a hotel, there are several things that you will want to communicate so that you can ensure you get the experience you want. Being able to communicate about things like the number of rooms, the number of nights, and the types of beds is very important.

Firstly, we will learn some basic terms concerning hotels and accomodations.

Hôtel, hotel

Une Auberge, a hostel

Lit, bed

Chambre, room

Lit à une place, twin bed

Lit simple, twin bed

Lit deux places, double bed

Grand lit deux places, queen size bed

Un Lit King Size, a king size bed

Un Lit superposé, a bunk bed

To begin, when you find a hotel that you would like to stay in, you will likely begin by asking them if they have any vacancies.

You can ask this by saying, *Avez-vous des chambres de disponible?* If they do, you can also ask them what rooms are available by saying, *Quelles chambres avez-vous de disponible?*

Before this, though, when you are walking around looking for a place to stay, you may see a sign outside that says *complet,* which means "no vacancy," or if they do have rooms available, you may see either *chambres de libres* or *de la place.* Both of these mean that the hotel has space available.

When you find a hotel, and they have rooms available, you can say the following phrases:

Je voudrais une chambre pour quatre. I'd like a room for four

Je voudrais une chambre dans l'espace fumeur s'il vous plaît. I would like a room in the smoking section, please.

S'il vous plaît donnez-moi une chambre avec une baignoire. Please give me a room with a bathtub.

Je voudrais rester dans une chambre avec un lit à une place. I would like to stay in a room with a twin bed.

Est-ce que votre hôtel offre le service en chambre? Does your hotel offer room service?

Cette auberge est-elle proche du quai du navire? Is this inn close to the ship dock?

Je voudrais une chambre non-fumeur s'il vous plaît. I would like a non-smoking room, please.

Le climatiseur est-il bon? Is the air conditioner good?

There may be some other interactions you would have with the front desk staff, like the following:

Once you have been assigned to a room and paid your cost, they will tell you, *Vous êtes dans la chambre numéro ____*. This means, "You are in room number ____."

They may tell you that *Vous devez régler la note avant midi.* Which is how we say, "You need to check out before noon" in French.

You may also need to cancel a booking you made. If this is the case, begin by saying, *je veux annuler ma reservation* or *"i want to cancel my reservation."* they will then ask you for your name, and you should be all set! You can say this either over the phone or in person.

More Useful Hotel Terms

La clé, the key

La clef, the key

Le premier étage, The first floor

Le deuxième étage, The second floor

Le troisième étage, The third floor

Le quatrième étage, The fourth floor

Où est l'ascenseur? Where is the elevator?

Où peux-je trouver la piscine? Where can I find a swimming pool?

L'ascenseur, the elevator

Où sont les escaliers? Where are the stairs?

Vocabulary List for Chapter 15

Hôtel, hotel

Une Auberge [oh-b-air-j], a hostel

Lit [l-ee], bed

Chambre [sh-om-b-ruh], room

Lit à une place [p-lah-s], twin bed

Grand [g-ron] lit deux places, queen size bed

Un Lit King Size, a king size bed

Un Lit superposé [soo-per-poh-z-ay], a bunk bed

Avez-vous des chambres de disponible [dee-s-poh-nee-b-luh]?

Complet [k-om-p-l-eh-t]

Chambres de libres [lee-b-ruh]

Le climatiseur est-il bon? Is the air conditioner good?

Je voudrais une chambre non-fumeur [noh-f-oo-m-uh-r]s'il vous plaît. I would like a non-smoking room, please.

S'il vous plaît donnez-moi une chambre avec une baignoire [bah-n-wah-ruh]. Please give me a room with a bathtub.

Je voudrais rester [r-es-tay] dans une chambre avec un lit à une place. I would prefer to stay in a room that features a twin bed.

Est-ce que votre hôtel offre [oh-f-ruh] le service en chambre? Does your hotel offer room service?

Je voudrais une chambre dans l'espace [l-ess-p-ah-s] fumeur. I would like a room in the smoking section.

Est-ce que cet hôtel est proche [p-roh-sh] a la gare [g-ah-ruh]? Is this hotel close to the train station?

Vous êtes dans la chambre numéro[noo-meh-ro] ____. You are in room number ____.

Vous devez [d-eh-vay] régler [r-eh-g-lay] la note [n-oh-t-uh]avant midi.

Nous voulons annuler [ah-noo-lay] notre réservation. We want to cancel our reservation.

La clé [k-lay], the key

La clef [k-l-eff], the key

Le premier [p-ruh-mee-eh-ruh] étage [ay-t-ah-j], the first floor

Le deuxième [duh-zee-eh-muh] étage, the second floor

Le troisième [t-r-wah-zee-eh-muh] étage, the third floor

Le quatrième [k-ah-t-ree-eh-muh] étage, the fourth floor

L'ascenseur [ah-son-sur], the elevator

Où [oo] est l'ascenseur? Where is the elevator?

Où sont [s-oh-n] les escaliers? Where are the stairs

Où se trouve [t-roo-v] la piscine [pee-see-nuh] ? Where is the swimming pool?

Chapter 16: At the Museum

As you may know, when visiting Europe or virtually any place in the world where French is spoken, there is a high chance that you will be visiting a museum at least once or twice. When you do so, there are some terms and phrases that will help you to get the most of your museum experience.

First, we will learn some general terms that pertain to art and a museum in general:

Une oeuvre, a work (usually describing art)

Une musée, a museum

Une œuvre d'art: a work of art

Une peinture, a painting

Une sculpture, a sculpture

Peindre, to paint

Un artefact, an artifact

Exposer ses tableaux, to exhibit one's arts

Un moyen d'expression artistique: an art form

Une exposition artistique, an artistic display / exhibition

Une brochure, a brochure

Un Opuscule, a pamphlet

Les beaux-arts, fine arts

Une exposition, an exhibition

Une peinture à l'huile, an oil painting

Un Peintre, a painter

Une peinture aquarelle: a watercolor painting

Now that you know how to say those words in French, we will look at how you can describe the art or the pieces of history in both positive and negative ways. The first set of words will be ones that you can use when you are really enjoying what you are looking at.

Positive Descriptors

Un chef-d'œuvre, a masterpiece

Je suis inspirée par quelque chose. I am inspired by something.

Je suis inspiré par quelqu'un. I am inspired by someone.

Très belle, very beautiful

Très intéressant(e), very interesting

exceptionnel(le), exceptional

Jolie, pretty / nice

Très réussi(e), well done

Remarquable, remarkable

Magnifique, magnificent

Extraordinaire, extraordinary

Impressionnant(e), impressive

Negative Descriptors

Simple, simple

Sans intérêt, dull / uninteresting

Modeste, modest,

Atroce, atrocious (this one is also a strong way to show distaste)

Affreux, awful (this is a very strong way to show distaste)

Inintéressant, uninteresting

Phrases

Now, we will look at some example sentences where you can use the words that you have learned so far in this chapter. These sentences will prove useful on your next trip to a French museum!

C'est une œuvre magnifique. It's a magnificent work!

Ce tableau est très intéressant. This piece is very interesting.

J'aime ce genre de peinture. I like this genre of painting.

Ce genre de peinture me plait. This type of painting pleases me.

Question:	*Comment vous trouvez ce peinture? What do you think of this painting?*
Answer:	*Il est très simple. It is very simple.*
Question:	*Qu'est-ce que vous pensez de cette sculpture? What do you think of this sculpture?*

Answer: *Je la trouve splendide. I find it to be splendid.*

Question: *Vous-aimez ce tableau? Do you like this piece?*

Question: *Ce tableau vous plaît? Does this piece please you?*

Answer: *Il m'inspire. It inspires me.*

Other things you may need to ask or to find when you are at a museum or any other tourist attraction are the following:

Les salles de bain, the bathrooms

Les toilettes, the toilets

La sortie, the exit

L'entrée, the entrance

La boutique de souvenirs, the gift shop

Vocabulary List for Chapter 16

Un musée [moo-say], a museum

Une œuvre [uh-v-ruh] d'art [d-ar] : a work of art

Une oeuvre, a work (usually describing art)

Un moyen [moh-yen] d'expression artistique: an art form

Une peinture [p-an-too-ruh], a painting

Une sculpture, a sculpture

Un artefact, an artifact

Une peinture [pah-n-too-ruh] à l'huile [l-oo-ee-luh], an oil painting

Peindre [pah-n-d-ruh], to paint

Une exposition [ex-poh-see-tee-on] artistique, an artistic display/exhibition

Une brochure, a brochure

Un Opuscule [oh-poo-s-koo-luh], a pamphlet

Les beaux-arts [boh-art], fine arts

Exposer ses tableaux [tah-b-loh], to exhibit one's arts

Un Peintre [pah-n-t-ruh], a painter

Une peinture aquarelle [ah-k-ah-reh-l], a watercolor painting

Un chef-d'œuvre [sh-ef-d-uh-v-ruh], a masterpiece

Je suis inspiré par quelque chose. I am inspired by something.

Quelque chose [k-el-k-uh][sh-oh-z]

Je suis inspiré par quelqu'un. I am inspired by someone.

Quelqu'un [k-el-k-uh-n]

Tres belle [b-eh-l], very beautiful

Jolie [j-oh-lee], Pretty / nice

Très intéressant(e), very interesting

[t-ray][ah-n-ter-ess-on-t]

Très réussi(e), well done

[ray-oo-see]

Extraordinaire, extraordinary

Remarquable, remarkable

Magnifique, magnificent

[mag-nee-fee-k]

exceptionnel(le), exceptional

Impressionnant(e), impressive

[ah-m-p-re-ss-ee-oh-n-on-tuh]

Modeste, modest

Simple, simple

[s-ah-m-p-luh]

Affreux [ah-f-ruh], awful

Sans intérêt [s-on-z][ah-n-t-eh-r-eh], dull / uninteresting

Atroce [ah-t-roh-s], atrocious

Inintéressant [ah-n-ah-n-t-eh-ress-on-t], uninteresting

Ce tableau est très intéressant. This piece is very interesting.
Tableau [t-ah-b-loh]

J'aime ce genre de peinture. I like this genre of painting.
Genre [j-on-ruh]

Ce genre de peinture me plaît. This type of painting pleases me.
Plaît [p-lay]

Question:	*Comment vous trouvez [t-roo-vay] ce peinture? What do you think of this painting?*
Answer:	*Il est très simple. It is very simple.*
Question:	*Qu'est-ce que vous pensez [p-oh-n-say] de cette sculpture? What do you think of this sculpture?*
Answer:	*Je la trouve splendide [s-p-loh-n-dee-d]. I find it to be splendid.*
Question:	*Vous-aimez [ah-may] ce [suh] tableau? Do you like this piece?*
Question:	*Ce tableau vous plaît? Does this piece please you?*
Answer:	*Il m'inspire [m-ah-n-sp-ee-ruh]. It inspires me.*

Les salles [sah-luh] de bain [bah-n], the bathrooms

Les toilettes, the toilets

La sortie [soh-r-tee], the exit

L'entrée [on-t-ray], the entrance

La boutique [boo-tee-k] de souvenirs, the gift shop

Chapter 17: Parts of the Body and Medical Emergency

Knowing the parts of the body can come in handy when playing sports, clothes shopping, seeing the doctor, and more. Learn how to talk about your body in French, from head to toe. We will begin with the parts of the body, and then we will look at going to the doctor and, finally, the phrases to help you in a medical emergency.

Parts of the Body

Le corps, the body

Les cheveux, hair. (In French, the word for hair is always plural, no matter what context it is found in. This is why "les" precedes it instead of *un or une.*)

La tête, the head

Un crâne, a skull

Le visage, face

L'œil, the eye

Les yeux, the eyes

Le nez , nose

Les joues, the cheeks

Une bouche, the mouth (*Une gueule* is another word for the mouth, but this one is reserved for more familiar conversations or those of a joking and teasing nature.)

Les lèvres, lips

Les dents, teeth

Langue, tongue

Une oreille, an ear

Un cou, a neck

Une gorge, a throat

La poitrine, the chest

Le cœur, the heart

Un estomac, a stomach

Un bras, an arm

Une épaule, a shoulder

Un coude, an elbow

Un poignet, a wrist

Une main, a hand

Un doigt, a finger

Un ongle, a fingernail

Un pouce, a thumb

Un dos, a back

Une jambe, a leg

Un genou, a knee

Une cheville, an ankle

Un pied, a foot

Un orteil, a toe

Verbs Involving the Body

Below are some verbs that you may use when talking about parts of the body.

Boire: to drink

Je bois avec ma langue

Lancer: to throw

Je lance le ballon avec mes mains. I throw the ball with my hands.

Sauter: to jump

Sophie saute avec ses jambes. Sophie jumps with her legs.

Courir: to run

Il court tres vite. He runs very fast.

Mâcher: to chew

Elle mâche très lentement. She chews very slowly.

Visiting the Doctor

When visiting the doctor, the following terms and phrases will help you to ensure you understand the doctor and that the doctor understands you as well. The following terms are things that you may need to tell the doctor about how you are feeling or things that they may ask you about how you are feeling. First, however, the doctor will likely ask you some questions in the form of a sentence when they first see you. Some common examples of this are below.

Qu'est-ce qui ne va pas? What's wrong?

Que sont vos symptômes? What are your symptoms?

Ou est-ce que c'est la douleur? Where is the pain?

Est-ce que cette partie est douloureuse? Is this part painful?

Est-ce que c'est correct si je vous touche ici? Is it okay if I touch you here?

Est-ce que vous êtes allergique à quelque chose? Are you allergic to something?

Question: *Est-ce que c'est la première fois que ceci vous est arrivé? Is this the first time this has happened to you?*

Answer: *Oui, yes* or *Non, no.*

After hearing one or more of these questions, you can answer with any of the following:

J'ai mal. I'm in pain.

Je ne vais pas bien. I'm not feeling well.

J'ai une Fièvre. I have a fever.

Bras / jambe / poignet brisée, broken arm/leg/wrist

Il y a du saignement. There is bleeding.

J'ai une blessure. I have an injury.

Il y a du gonflement. There is swelling.

Je pense qu'il a une Maladie. I think he has a sickness (or an illness).

Words and Phrases for a Medical Emergency

In a medical emergency, it can be hard to remember a language that is not your first. Remember the following few phrases just in case you are ever in this situation.

Au secours! Help!

Aidez-moi. Help me.

J'ai besoin d'une ambulance. I need an ambulance.

Urgence, the Emergency Room

Il y avait un accident. There was an accident.

L'Hôpital, the hospital

Je pense que j'ai besoin d'un médecin. I think I need a doctor.

S'il vous plaît, laissez-moi voir un médecin. *Please, let me see a doctor.*

Une trousse de premiers secours, a first-aid kit

Below are some phrases that you may hear the doctor asking you in an emergency. They may also tell you some of these things as a statement.

Qui dois-je contacter? Who should I contact?

Vous avez... You have...

Mon diagnostique est... My diagnosis is...

Prenez votre médicament ____ fois par jour pendant _____ jours. Take your medication _____ times a day for _____ days.

Sang, blood

Assurance médicale, medical insurance

Un bleu, a bruise

Diagnostic, diagnosis

Une Infirmière, a female nurse

Un infirmier, a male nurse

Une pharmacie, a pharmacy

Une Radiographie, an X-ray

Une Pilule, a pill

Vocabulary List for Chapter 17

Le corps [k-or], the body

Les cheveux [sh-uh-v-uh], hair

La tête [t-eh-t], the head

Un crâne [k-rah-nuh], a skull

Le visage [vee-z-ah-j], face

L'œil [oy], the eye

Les yeux [y-uh], the eyes

Le nez [nay], nose

Les joues [j-oo], the cheeks

Une bouche [b-oo-sh], a mouth.

Une gueule [g-uh-luh]

Les lèvres [l-eh-v-ruh], lips

Les dents [d-on-t], teeth

Une oreille [oh-ray], an ear

Un cou [k-oo], a neck

Une gorge [g-oh-r-j], a throat

La poitrine [p-wah-t-ree-n], the chest

Le cœur [k-uh-r], the heart

Un estomac [ess-toh-mah-k], a stomach

Un bras [b-rah], an arm

Une épaule [ay-poh-luh], a shoulder

Un coude [k-oo-d], an elbow

Un poignet [p-wah-n-y-ay], a wrist

Une main [m-ah-n], a hand

Un doigt [d-wah], a finger

Un ongle [oh-n-g-luh], a fingernail

Un pouce [poo-s], a thumb

Un dos [doh], a back

Une jambe [j-ah-m-b], a leg

Un genou [j-uh-noo], a knee

Une cheville [sh-uh-vee], an ankle

Un pied [pee-yay], a foot

Un orteil [oh-r-tay], a toe

Boire [b-wah-r]: to drink

Je bois avec ma langue [l-oh-n-g-uh]

Lancer [l-oh-n-say]: to throw

Je lance le ballon avec mes mains. I throw the ball with my hands.

Sauter [s-oh-tay]: to Jump

Sophie saute avec ses jambes. Sophie jumps with her legs.

Courir [k-oo-ree-r]: to run

Il court très vite. He runs very fast.

Mâcher [mah-sh-ay]: to chew

Elle mâche très lentement. She chews very slowly.

Qu'est-ce qui ne va pas? What's wrong?

Que sont [soh-n-t] vos [voh] symptômes? What are your symptoms?

Où est-ce que c'est le douleur [doo-luh-r]? Where is the pain?

Est-ce que ça fait mal [m-ah-l]? Does this hurt?

Est-ce que je peux [p-uh] vous [v-oo] toucher [too-shay] ici? Can I touch you here?

Question: *Est-ce que c'est la première fois que ceci [suh-see] vous est arrivé? Is this the first time this has happened to you?*
Answer: *Oui, yes or Non, no.*

Est-ce que vous avez [ah-vay] des allergies? Do you have any allergies?

J'ai mal. I'm in pain.
Je ne vais [v-ay] pas [pah] bien [bee-yen]. I'm not feeling well.
Bras / jambe / poignet brisée, broken arm/leg/wrist
Il y a du saignement [say-nuh-mon], There is bleeding.
J'ai une blessure [b-leh-soo-ruh]. I have an injury.
J'ai une Fièvre [fee-eh-v-ruh]. I have a fever.
Il y a du gonflement [gon-f-luh-mon]. There is swelling.

Je pense [poh-n-suh] qu'il a une Maladie [mah-lah-dee]. I think he has a sickness (an illness).

Au secours [seh-k-oo-r]! Help!

Aidez-moi [ay-day-m-wah]. Help me.

Urgence [oo-r-j-on-suh], the Emergency Room

Il y avait un accident. There was an accident.

L'Hôpital, the hospital

J'ai besoin [b-eh-z-wah-n] d'une ambulance. I need an ambulance.

S'il vous plaît, laissez-moi voir un médecin. Please, let me see a doctor.

Ou est-ce que je peux [puh] trouver une clinique [k-lee-nee-k] médicale? Where is the nearby hospital?

Une trousse [t-roo-suh] de premiers [p-ruh-mee-air] secours [seh-koo-r], a first-aid kit

Qui dois-je [d-wah-j] contacter [k-on-tah-k-tay]? Who should I contact?

Vous [voo] avez [ah-vay]... You have...

Mon diagnostique [dee-ag-noh-s-t-eek] est... My diagnosis is...

Prenez [p-r-uh-nay] votre médicament [m-eh-dee-k-ah-mon] ____ fois par jour pendant ____ jours. Take your medication ____ times a day for ____ days.

Sang [s-on-g], blood

Assurance [ah-soo-ron-s] médicale, medical insurance

Un bleu, a bruise

Diagnostic, Diagnosis

Une Infirmiere [ah-n-f-eh-r-me-air], a female nurse

Un infirmier, a male nurse

Une pharmacie [f-ah-r-mah-see], a pharmacy

Une Radiographie [rah-dee-oh-g-rah-f-ee], an X-ray

Une Pilule [prr-loo-l], a pill

Chapter 18: Hobbies, Games, and Sports

In this chapter, we will switch gears a little bit and talk about a fun topic: games and sports! These terms will be useful for you in social situations like if you are going out with your new French friends or if you are looking for something related to your hobby in a French-speaking place.

Hobbies

This section will teach you words that involve hobbies and examples of sentences so that you can see how to use them in practice.

Les passe-temps, hobbies

La cuisine, cooking

Le crochet, crocheting

Des mots croisés, crossword puzzles

La danse, dancing

La pêche, fishing

Le jardinage, gardening

La chasse, hunting

La randonnée, hiking

Un puzzle, a puzzle

Le tricot, knitting

Un film, movie

La musique, music

La peinture, painting

La lecture, reading

La couture, sewing

La télévision, television

Marie aime regarder la télévision. Marie likes watching television.

Ma mère fait le tricot. My mother knits.

Je fais de la pêche avec mon frère. I fish with my brother.

Je suis expert à faire les puzzles. I'm expert at doing puzzles.

Games

This section includes games and includes example sentences at the end, as well.

Les jeux, games

Les jeux de société, board games

Les jeux de cartes, card games

Le jeu de dames, checkers

Les échecs, chess

Les fléchettes, darts

Le billard, pool

Les jeux vidéo, video games

Les jeux de lettres, word games

Je joue aux jeux de sociétés avec toute ma famille les lundis soirs. I play board games with my whole family on Monday nights.

Il est très fructueux quand il joue au billard. He is very successful when he plays pool.

Mon frère joue aux jeux vidéo pendant toute la journée. My brother plays video games all day.

J'aime jouer aux fléchettes au bistro avec mes amis. I like playing darts at the bar with my friends.

Sports

This section includes the most common sports and words that would be associated with them, as well as some example sentences.

Les Sports [lay][spo-r], sports

Soccer/Le foot, soccer

Football Américain, football

Le basket, basketball

Un Ballon, a ball

Frisbee, frisbee

Le jogging, jogging

La voile, sailing

Le cyclisme / le vélo, cycling

La boxe, boxing

Le hockey, hockey

Le ski, skiing

La natation, swimming

Le Tennis, tennis

La lutte, wrestling

Courir (verb), to run

Le gazon, grass

Terrain de jeu, field

Serena Williams est le meilleur joueur de tennis au monde. Serena williams is the best tennis player in the world.

Elle est très vite quand elle participe dans des concours de natation. She is very fast when she participates in swimming races.

Je sens libre quand je fais du vélo. I feel free when I am biking.

Le football américain peut être très dangereux. Football can be very dangerous.

Vocabulary List for Chapter 18

Les passe-temps [p-ah-s-t-oh-m-p], hobbies

La cuisine [k-wee-z-ee-n], cooking

Le crochet [k-roh-sh-ay], crocheting

Des mots croisés [m-oh][k-r-wah-z-ay], crossword puzzles

La danse [d-on-s], dancing

La pêche [p-e-sh], fishing

Le jardinage [j-ar-dee-n-ah-j], gardening

La chasse [sh-ah-s], hunting

La randonnée [r-oh-n-d-oh-n-ay], hiking

Un puzzle [poo-z-l], a puzzle

Le tricot [t-ree-k-oh], knitting

Un film [f-ee-l-m], movie

La musique [moo-zee-k], music

La peinture, painting

La lecture [l-ek-too-r], reading

La couture [koo-too-ruh], sewing

La télévision [tay-lay-vee-zee-on], television

Marie aime [eh-m] regardé la télévision. Marie likes watching television.

Ma mère fait [f-eh] le tricot. My mother knits.

Je fais de la pêche avec [ah-v-eh-k] mon frère. I fish with my brother.

Je suis [s-wee] expert [ex-p-eh-r] à faire les puzzles. I'm expert at doing puzzles.

Les jeux [j-uh], games
Les jeux de société [soh-see-eh-tay], board games
Les jeux de cartes [k-ah-r-tuh], card games
Le jeu de dames [d-ah-muh], checkers
Les échecs [ay-sh-eh-k], chess
Les fléchettes [f-l-eh-sh-eh-tuh], darts
Le billard, pool
Les jeux vidéo [vee-day-oh], video games
Les jeux de lettres [l-eh-t-ruh], word games

Je joue [j-oo] aux jeux de sociétés avec toute [t-oo-t] ma famille [fah-mee] les lundis soirs. I play board games with my whole family on Monday nights.

Il est très fructueux [f-roo-k-too-uh] quand [k-on] il joue au billard. He is very successful when he plays pool.

Mon frère joue aux jeux vidéo pendant [p-on-d-on] toute la journée. My brother plays video games all day.

J'aime jouer aux fléchettes au bistro [bee-s-t-roh] avec mes [m-eh-z] amis. I like playing darts at the bar with my friends.

Les Sports [lay][spo-r], sports

Soccer/Le foot [f-uh-t], soccer

Football Américain, football

Le basket, basketball

Un Ballon [b-ah-loh-n], a ball

Frisbee, Frisbee

Courir (verb) [k-oo-ree-r], to run

Le gazon [luh][gah-z-on], Grass

Terrain de jeu [t-air-an][duh][j-uh], field

Le jogging, jogging

La voile [v-wah-l], sailing

Le cyclisme [see-k-lee-z-muh] / le vélo, cycling

La boxe, boxing

Le hockey, hockey

Le ski, Skiing

La natation [nah-tah-see-on], swimming

Le Tennis, tennis

La lutte [l-oo-tuh], wrestling

Serena Williams est le meilleur [may-uh-r] joueur [j-oo-uh-r] de tennis au monde [m-oh-n-d]. Serena williams is the best tennis player in the world.

Elle est très vite [v-ee-t] quand elle participe [pah-r-tee-see-p] *dans des concours [k-on-k-oo-r] de natation.* She is very fast when she participates in swimming races.

Je sens [s-ah-n] libre [l-ee-b-ruh] quand [k-on] je fais du vélo. I feel free when I am biking.

Le football américain peut [p-uh] être très dangereux [d-on-j-uh-r-uh]. Football can be very dangerous.

Chapter 19: Conversations About the Future

In this final chapter of the book, we will learn the terms and phrases that will help you when talking about the future. This theme is quite fitting for the end of the book as you will then be able to use these in conjunction with all of the others in this book, going forward into your future endeavors.

Future Verbs

I will begin by giving you some common verbs that you can use and that you can combine with some of the words you now know so that you can talk about your future wishes, desires, or hopes.

Je Veux ____. I want

Je Voudrais ____. I would like ____

J'Aimerais ____. I would like ____

The difference among the three examples above is that the first one is used for friends and in more casual conversations, while the second two would be used more formally, usually among people whom you don't know well.

Je souhaite ____. I wish

Je te souhaite _____. I wish for you (casual / familiar)

Je vous souhaite ____. I wish for you (formal / respectful)

J'espère ____. I hope

Je jouerais. I will play

J'irai. I will go

Je Finirais. I will finish

J'appellerai. I will call

J'aurais. I will have

J'enverrais. I will send

Je ferais. I will do

Je saurais. I will know

Je verrais. I will see

Future Sentences

We will now use some of these verbs in example sentences so that once you are familiar with them, you will be able to use them in conversations about the future, such as "I will go to school."

1. *Vous aimeriez déjeuner avec moi demain?* Are you interested in getting lunch tomorrow with me?
2. *Vous aimeriez dîner avec moi la semaine prochaine?* Would you like to get dinner with me next week?
3. *Est-ce que tu veux aller prendre un verre après le travail?* Do you want to go get a drink after work?

4. *Est-ce que tu veux boire un coup, après le travail?* Do you want to drink one after work?

Notice how the four sentences above are similar in what they are saying. However, the first two would be used for someone you don't know too well and whom you want to ask in a respectful way. The third and fourth demonstrate the way that you would ask someone who you are friends with whom you regularly spend time with.

Je te souhaite une bonne journée. I wish you a good day.
Je souhaite aller au Canada. I wish to go to Canada.
J'irai à l'école. I will go to school
Je t'appellerais demain. I will call you tomorrow.
J'espère que vous êtes heureux. I hope you are happy.
Je finirais mon petit déjeuner après cet appel. I will finish my breakfast after this call.
Je te verrais dans un mois. I will see you in one month.

In French, if we want to say, "see you later," we would say, *à toute à l'heure* . If you want to say "see you later" on a specific day, we would say, "see you Tuesday," meaning, *à mardi*, for example.

Vocabulary List for Chapter 19

Je Veux [v-uh] ____ , I want

J'Aimerais [ah-meh-ray] ____ , I would like ____

Je Voudrais [voo-d-ray] ____ , I would like ____

Je souhaite [soo-het] ____ , I wish

Je te [tuh] souhaite ____ , I wish for you (casual / familiar)

Je vous [voo] souhaite ____ , I wish for you (formal / respectful)

J'espère [ess-pair] ____ I hope

Je jouerais [joo-ur-ay] , I will play

J'irai [ee-ray] , I will go

Je Finirais [fee-nee-ray], I will finish

J'appellerai [ah-peh-l-er-ay], I will call

J'aurais [oh-ray] , I will have

J'enverrais [on-v-air-ay] , I will send

Je ferais [f-uh-ray], I will do

Je saurais [s-oh-ray], I will know

Je verrais [v-uh-ray], I will see

Vous aimeriez déjeuner [day-j-uh-nay] avec moi [m-wah] demain? Would you like to get lunch with me tomorrow?

Vous aimeriez dîner [dee-nay] avec moi la semaine prochaine? Would you like to get dinner with me next week?

Est-ce que tu veux [v-uh] aller prendre [p-ron-d-ruh] un verre [v-air] après [ah-pray] le travail? Do you want to go get a drink after work?

Est-ce que tu veux boire [b-wah-ruh] un coup [k-oo], après le travail? Do you want to drink one after work?

Je te souhaite une bonne journée. I wish you a good day.

Je souhaite aller au [oh] Canada. I wish to go to Canada.

J'irai à l'école [l-ay-k-oh-luh]. I will go to school

Je t'appellerais [t-ah-pel-uh-ray] demain. I will call you tomorrow.

J'espère que vous êtes [eh-t-uh] heureux [uh-r-uh]. I hope you are happy.

Je finirais mon petit déjeuner après ce [s-eh-tuh] appel [ah-p-el]. I will finish my breakfast after this call.

Je te verrais dans un mois [m-wah]. I will see you in one month.

À toute à l'heure [ah][too-t][ah][l-err]

À mardi! [ah][mah-r-dee].

Conclusion

Thank you for reaching the end of *Learn French With Common Phrases*. I hope that after reading this book, you feel more ready than you ever to go forth and use your French knowledge in new places and with new people. The phrases and words contained within this book will equip you for almost any encounter and situation where you would need these French language skills. I hope this makes you feel more confident going into your travels and well-prepared for anything unexpected. With the skills you have developed from reading this book, you might just become the French speaker in the family or group. Your knowledge will ensure that you get what you want and need, or that you understand what is happening if you ever need to see a doctor when you are in a French-speaking country. Through your knowledge of the language, you can confidently book a hotel with the right type of amenities and services for yourself or your group.

Continue to practice your pronunciation of the terms and phrases in this book, and challenge yourself to develop your own sentences from the tools that this book has given you. Mixing and matching the words and verbs that you have learned in this book will allow you to create virtually any sentence you need when it comes to conversation. Even if you are able to read the signs or websites that you come across in French while planning a trip or while away in a French-speaking country, this knowledge will have proved to benefit you greatly!

If you are looking for what steps to take next, it would be to continue to expose yourself to as many new French words as possible! Listen to French podcasts, watch French films, or engage in as many conversations in French as you can. This will help to keep this French knowledge fresh in your brain and will solidify it in your memory. Doing so will help you to keep this for as long as possible, hopefully for the rest of your life. There is never too much practice that you can have when it comes to learning a language. If you like, you can continue to read this book and spend extra time on the vocabulary pages of each section to get your pronunciation as clear and accurate as possible. If you read this book out loud the first time, continue to read it in this fashion, and if you did not, make sure you read it aloud at least once. This will be extremely beneficial for your comprehension of the language and the longevity of the language pronunciation in your memory.

Now, use what you have learned and become a French conversationalist. With an entirely new language under your belt, pick up as much information and knowledge as you can along the way. This book will be available to you the entire time, just in case you need to flip back for a little tune-up.

If you found this book useful in any way, a review on Amazon is always appreciated!

Thank you.

Paul Irving